D1203511

The Edge of April

THE EDGE OF APRIL

A *Biography of* JOHN BURROUGHS

HILDEGARDE HOYT SWIFT

Illustrated by LYND WARD

WILLIAM MORROW AND COMPANY
New York · 1957

Second Printing, August, 1958

© 1957 by Hildegarde Hoyt Swift.

Printed in the United States of America.

Library of Congress Catalog Card No. 57-8563

DEDICATION

To all lovers of the wilderness
Who know
The feel of a forest trail,
Thrush song at evening,
The joy of a mountain top,
This book is dedicated
by the author.

Foreword

We feel very fortunate when we have the chance to become acquainted with distinguished men and women, for everyone enjoys meeting interesting people.

In my own case, though I did see a good deal of my grandfather when I was a child, I was too young then to appreciate fully the opportunity I had. Of those childhood days, nevertheless, I have many happy memories. There were walks through the fields below Woodchuck Lodge, when we looked for birds' nests in the grass; picnics at Slabsides when he broiled for us his "brigand steaks" over the coals. Up near the Old Homestead he showed us the pool where he had obtained his slate pencils as a boy and we waded there in the cool water just as he had years before. At Riverby he helped us pick cherries and let us play among the vine-covered bean poles in his garden.

One summer we visited him at Woodchuck Lodge in early July. It was the Fourth and we had arrived at his house in the mountains without any fireworks. "Nothing for the children to celebrate with?" he asked in a troubled voice. "I'll see what I can do about that." So he put the three of us in his little Ford and together we drove to the village. There was disappointment at first: the stores had none for sale. I remember that he tried to explain to us that there was some sort of ban, which he thought foolishness; but he was not to be daunted, and he was as delighted as we were when at last he was able to locate some Roman candles and sparklers. "We'll have our celebration, after all," he exclaimed, as he came out of the store with his bundles. We bore them off in triumph to Woodchuck Lodge, and as soon as it was dark on the mountain he helped us set them off.

My grandfather never seemed to lose his understanding of a child's world. We shall always remember, as an instance of this, his ready and complete sympathy when we lost our beloved little terrier; how he talked to us of his own experience when two of his dogs had been killed, tragically like ours, in accidents; how he consoled and comforted us.

That our grandfather was famous, even as children we soon knew. There were the newspaper photographers who came to take pictures of us with him on his birthday, and the many other visitors, expected and unexpected, who appeared at our home. One of these was Henry Ford, who each year presented him with a new automobile gleaming with nickel trim. My grandfather was too much of a nature lover to be a good driver, however, for he was apt to be attracted by what he saw—by birds, for example—and forget the wheel. There was the time he and his three grandchildren—Ursula, John, and I—were nearly annihilated together. He drove his Ford part way through the side of the old barn at Woodchuck Lodge and there it hung, with us in it, precariously perched over space, for the barn was at the edge of a hill.

Though my grandfather spent much time in his later years at Woodchuck Lodge, he always returned to Riverby. One would be apt to find him in the summer-house, in the rocking chair with the broad arms which served as a desk. Here he would sit with his pencil and his note pad. In front of him were the green vineyards, the river, and the wooded slopes beyond; and his eyes would gaze at these as he jotted down from time to time his thoughts as they came.

It has been my privilege to have these associations, and the most intense personal feelings are linked with them. Nevertheless, I can feel objectively about my grandfather, too, and be proud of him, not for family reasons alone, but for what he was: a truly great American.

The boy trudging through the snow-filled fields, trying to earn money for books, thwarted, discouraged by his family, who, in spite of all the odds against him, made a literary career for himself and became the recipient of honorary university degrees, the friend of the great of his day, a member of the American Academy of Arts and Letters, loved by thousands for whom he made the world a richer place—this is the man about whom you are going to read.

ELIZABETH BURROUGHS

Riverby, West Park, New York
October, 1956

Introduction

The events I have used in this biography of John Burroughs are in every case factual—taken from the man's own memories, from the recollections of his son and grandchildren, the recording of his secretary—or revealed in the letters of friends. The discovery of a dead tanager, the failure to shoot a red fox while hunting on the mountain, or the finding of an unknown bird in the Deacon woods—these are simple but formative incidents in the early life of the great naturalist, as he himself acknowledged them to be.

This story of John Burroughs is dramatized, not fictionized, for there is no fabrication in the pattern of my book; rather, I feel, it presents the truth. Certainly I have chosen special events and incidents, eliminating others, and tried to weld them into a progressive narrative, without benefit of correspondence, critiques, or marginal notes —all the paraphernalia with which some biographers endow their creations, and under which they so often bury their subject until there is neither breath in the body nor life in the bones.

I believe that John Burroughs himself would have approved of this approach to his life, for he used a similar one in his study of nature. In his introduction to *Wake-Robin* he wrote:

"The Literary Naturalist does not take liberties with the facts; facts are the flora upon which he lives. The more and fresher the facts, the better. I can do nothing without them, but I must give them my own flavor. I must impart to them a quality which heightens and intensifies them.

"To *interpret* Nature is not to improve upon her; it is to draw her out; it is to have an emotional intercourse with her, absorb her, and reproduce her tinged with the color of the spirit. If I name every bird I see in my walk, describe its color and ways, etc., give a lot of facts or details about the bird, it is doubtful if my reader is interested. But if I relate the bird in some way to human life—show what it is to me and what it is to the landscape and the season—then do I give my reader a live bird and not a labeled specimen."

Much in the same way I have tried to give a living man, not a labeled specimen; to build in my reader a sense of friendship with the great artist, the incorruptible and incomparable lover of life that was John Burroughs.

William M. Sloane, President of the American Academy of Arts and Letters, said in his final tribute, "In all American Literature there was but one John Burroughs." Earlier, Theodore Roosevelt wrote, with a simplicity which the staunch "Oom John" must have liked, "It is good for our people that you were born."

Surely a sense of friendship with such a man is important and rewarding. At least, I have found it so; and out of my discovery of the man, John Burroughs, this biography is written.

HILDEGARDE H. SWIFT

November 1, 1956

Part One

1837-1854

There was a child went forth every day,
And the first object he look'd upon, that object he became,
And that object became part of him for the day or a certain part
 of the day,
Or for many years . . .
The early lilacs became part of this child,
And grass, and white and red morning-glories, and white and red
 clover, and the song of the phoebe-bird,
And the Third-month lambs and the sow's pink-faint litter, and
 the mare's foal and the cow's calf,
And the noisy brood of the barnyard or by the mire of the
 pond-side,
And the fish suspending themselves so curiously below there, and
 the beautiful curious liquid,
And the water-plants with their graceful flat heads, all became
 part of him.

WALT WHITMAN

Chapter 1

"OLLY ANN, OLLY ANN, WAKE UP!"

Her own name! Somewhere—where was it? But it was still dark; half awake she listened for a moment. Then the mists of sleep swirled round her and the lure of the soft feather bed pulled her back.

"Olly Ann! Hurry up, Olly Ann!"

It was Pa, of course. Who else would holler like that? Whatever he wanted, whatever you did, he always hollered. Then she remembered. 'Twas probably Ma who needed her. Quickly she pulled on her spun-yarn stockings and felt her way round the spool-like bedposts, stooping at last to pull the covers back over little Jane. Then she pushed open the door into the big, cold kitchen.

Pa was stooped on one knee, blowing up the sparks in the wide fireplace. Puff, whine, puff! The bellows seemed to labor complainingly. But now the kindling caught and soon the big logs would answer.

"Can I go to Ma now?"

"No, you tend to things here, Olly Ann. Fill the biggest kettle full and have the water hot. Hiram's rid for the doctor; he'll be here any minute. Don't worry, child!" He stood up now and touched the little girl's shoulder gently. "Ma's all right. A birthing ain't a sickness."

"What else can I do, Pa?"

"Light a tallow dip, an' keep the fire brisk. Where'd your mother store her oldest homespun?"

"Third drawer down th' dresser." Olly Ann waved a hand back toward the shadows. There in the corner stood the old mahogany bureau, thick and ponderous and someway reassuring. Only yesterday, it seemed, she had sat on top of it and kicked her heels, "nothin' but a baby," safely out of the way while Ma worked. She could see Ma plain, running the long wooden shovel into the brick oven, inching out the loaves—gently, oh so gently. Um . . . the good fresh smell of new hot rye bread!

Yes, she had been the baby then. Since, there'd been Wilson, Curtis, Edmund, Jane. But little Edmund had hardly stayed at all. Tonight—boy or girl, she wondered. She hoped a girl, someone to side with Jane and her and take their part!

She stooped over the wood box and chose more kindling with care. Birch, for it snaps up fastest, she thought. She pushed the kettle back on the big crane, dipping one finger in to test the water's warmth. She stood by the fire, tense and listening, a tall, slender nine-year-old with anxious brown eyes.

Why don't Doc come?

The sharp klop of hoofs pounding up the hard roadway seemed to answer her worry. There came a "Whoa" and a thump, and now the doctor, as if propelled into the room bodily by the brisk April breeze. Cheerful and unconcerned, he pinched her cheek and praised her industry.

"Up early, Sister Martha! Everything ready? A good fire. Plenty of hot water. Fine, as far as it goes. But how about some coffee and a bowl of Injun mush?"

Oh, she'd forgotten breakfast! Ma wouldn't have.

"My name's not Martha," she said soberly.

"Olly, Olly Ann. To be sure, my dear! How could I have forgotten it so soon? Only the other day I came to bring you in my old black satchel."

That's nonsense, she told herself, as she fetched another kettle and stirred Indian meal into some of the boiling water, just a silly grown-up joke. I know how babies come. The day before yesterday two of the ewes had their lambs, so tiny and wobbly. Didn't I watch and help Pa?

The hours passed. Soon thin morning light filtered through the small leaded panes of the window in the birthing room. Outside, the April breeze lifted a branch of the big pine, scratching its needles softly against the glass. From the top of it an early highhole sent down his triumphant, two-toned call. Wick, wick! Wick, wick! Wick, wick! From inside the room came the first gasping, reedy cry of a newborn child!

Chauncey Burroughs took his little son into his work-worn hands. Suddenly his eyes misted with unexpected tears. Bone of his bone, and flesh of his flesh. He held him steadily, gazing down at him with gladness and pride.

The woman in the bed stirred, sighing a little. Her eyes opened. She looked up at the man questioningly. Then she stretched up her arms and he stooped down, placing the baby by her side.

"All's well, darlin'," he said. "A fine boy! Glad I be 'tis a man child—another pair of hands to help me with the farm!"

"A man child." A pair of hands indeed! What a way to think on't! As if he were a horse or ox or beast of burden. A mind and heart and soul to love and cherish, her little son!

Gently she smoothed one hand over the tiny, well-shaped head, already misted with soft reddish hair, then drew him close, and closer still. Exaltation and happiness seemed to flow through her veins, a sense of triumph and joy. Had she ever known this feeling before? Hiram, Olly Ann, little Jane—all the others she had longed for and welcomed. But waiting for this seventh child there seemed to be a special love.

Something of the old tales of her childhood, the old superstitions of her Celtic forbears came to her now. To the Irish the seventh child might even be fey, might have the gift of second sight. He would know more, feel more, see more. She could almost hear her father saying, "He'll be th' lucky one!"

So little Johnny Burroughs was born to Chauncey and Amy Kelly Burroughs on the third of April, 1837, on a farm in the western part of the Catskill country of New York State.

On the day when he arrived other things new were coming into life, from the opening red buds of the maples to the new lambs bleating in the shed. All the day before, his father had been tapping the fresh sweetness of the sugar bush, driving spiles into the big maples so that their pungent sap could run out into the buckets.

On the day when Johnny Burroughs arrived, bluebirds and robins were returning to the mountain country, phoebes were looking for their old nesting sites, and from the big pine in back of the house came the frequent whiplash call of the flicker.

There was a new warmth in the air, which still held an edge of cold, just as the fields were bare, with only a thin line of snow along the stone walls and up through the woods.

New life replacing the dying winter. It was a good time to be born.

How old he was when he first noticed the mountain, John Burroughs never knew. As long as he could remember, it had been a part of his life, big and towering and beautiful, looking down at him. Later on he wrote, "Old Clump, out of whose loins I sprang," as if the mountain had been father and mother to him, as it was early comrade and friend.

The Burroughs' farm climbed one high shoulder of it, and rambled down into deep, fertile bottom lands on either side. In the rich valleys rye and wheat and corn stood high in season. On the hillside cows and sheep found ready pasturage.

Johnny was a noticing child. He liked to stand at the window of the back bedroom in the morning to see whether gray, swirling mists still hid his mountain. At night he looked for its great, rounded shape, sharp and clear against the sky. Johnny noticed other things, too— the ways of people, whether kind or unkind, hurried or quiet. Pa, he thought, never stopped to *look*. Loud-voiced and busy, he racketed in and out of the house, shouting his orders, scolding the boys, telling the hired man "He'd better! Yes, siree!" or blaming Ma if the pork stew was cold.

But Ma was different. Ma was gentle and slow and steady, and sometimes she acted as if she were somewhere else. When the big boys were rough and unruly and Pa was rude, she would go to the door and look out for a long time at the mountain. When she came back, her blue-gray eyes were filled with a quiet light.

Wherever in the world was Johnny? Amy Kelly Burroughs came through the door of the buttery. She wiped her hands on the roller towel that hung democratically for everyone by the door, glancing anxiously about the kitchen. Wherever had he gotten to? She had left him rocking little Eden to sleep in the low, blue cradle, and the baby was asleep fast enough, she could see that. This was a task which Johnny would always do. None of the other boys could have been depended upon at his age, but her Johnny could! Sitting on the edge of the cradle, he rocked himself along with the baby, till sometimes she found them both asleep. But today he was simply—gone.

Swiftly she looked in all the "hidey" places. Was he in the little back bedroom beyond her bedroom? No! Could he have crawled into the oven beside the fireplace? He'd be pot-black if he had. But no!

Worried now, Amy Burroughs snatched her sunbonnet from the spool peg where it hung, started out the door and down the stone steps in front. "Johnny," she called, with rising tension, "Johnny!" After all, he was only four.

The little boy had grown tired rocking his small brother to sleep. What good were babies anyway? Why didn't the other children come back from school? It was stupid staying here alone. What should he play with now? Look for crickets on the hearth, the nice, long-horned ones he liked? Wouldn't be there till the heat brought them out tonight most likely. He'd go to school next year, Ma said. Could go now. Didn't he know his A already, two long legs joined at the top? He knew what he'd do. He'd play outdoors.

Quickly he pushed open the front door and climbed down the stonework. Cuff, the mastiff, a lazy mass of yellow, picked himself up from his place against the stone and sniffed at Johnny wonderingly. Then he followed along. On and on and on, sturdy legs hurried. Past the big barn now, up and up the hill—way up, to the place where the road turned. He had one impulse—to run away. To run and run and run. My, how big he was! Almost as big as Hi, the oldest of them all. Most a man growed, mebbe, going off all by himself, going all alone. For a brief moment he strutted proudly. He puffed, too, for he had climbed and climbed.

Here was another little path going into the woods. Better try this. Berry bushes reached for him. Long, snaky briars tore his spun-yarn stockings. They tripped and tired him. He was trudging along the Deacon Road now. Hot and weary, he was going more slowly. Then a curious thing happened. From somewhere close beside him a shrill whistle sounded, sudden and someway frightening. Were the boys hiding there at the edge of the woods? No, no one, no one at all. Again the shrill, demanding whistle. Little

Johnny looked up. A great bird was swooping above him in ever-lowering circles, a huge red-shouldered hawk riding the air in mighty loops. Was he coming for him? As he flew, a great black shadow careened across the ground beside the little boy.

Frightened, Johnny ran to the stone wall that followed the path and held the woods in check. He crouched beside it, hardly daring to look. Cuff crawled in next to him, touching him gently with a wet, slippery nose, trying to offer comfort. How long he waited, panic-stricken and trembling! Then when he looked up, the big bird was gone.

Where was his home? Could he ever find it? Way down at the foot of the hill, how little and far away it looked—miles and miles away. Could he reach it? He must try. He must hurry, hurry, hurry, or mebbe—he would never see it again.

Falling, picking himself up and struggling on down, little Johnny came home, back to the place of sensible blue sunbonnets and his mother's loving arms.

Always in later years he remembered this first time he heard the call to run away, and this first time he felt the passionate need of home. All his life John Burroughs was torn between these two desires, the deep, underlying need for peace, set against the urgent zest for fresh adventure, which was to carry him further and further along his Deacon Road.

Chapter 2

AMY KELLY, AS HER OLD FRIENDS STILL CALLED HER, came through the bedroom door, holding Johnny by the right hand and baby Eden in the crook of her left arm. The baby crowed and laughed as Johnny shrieked and capered beside them, like a colt just loose in the pasture.

"School, school, school!" he chanted. "I'm going to school today, today, today!"

Wasn't he five years old just recently, with maple sugar and all? And now he was going off with the big fellows, grown up at last. He looked down at his new blue-and-white-striped suit proudly and capered again. Ma had made it at night by the light of her tallow dip. As he jumped, the small extra pieces on each shoulder—"ep-lets" Ma called them—jumped and capered too.

"Wal, Johnny!" said Chauncey Burroughs, who was sitting at the end of the long trestle table. He stretched out one hand, still holding a piece of pie, and waved it. "Come sit here by Pa and eat your breakfast. Got to feed that big brain o' yours!" He smiled for once and thought of the years when he himself had taught school and little fel-

lows like this had come to him. As for the big ones, some
of them had known more than he did, at that! But if they
showed it, he knew how to quiet them!

"Who'll take Johnny to school?" asked his mother, easing the baby into his high chair. "You, Olly Ann?"

"Not me," said Olly Ann, sliding sidewise off the long
bench and wiping her mouth elegantly on the back of her
hand. " 'Prompt today,' Teacher said. I ought to be there
now. Oh, Ma, I can't—really." Her first firm tone changed
into a whine, and she eyed her mother with a tragic face.
"Johnny'd just take hours!"

"Me, me, me," shrieked Jane, banging the table for attention, but Amy Burroughs ignored her. By herself she
was a good child, but with Johnny . . . what a notorious
team they were! Only last year they had tried to roll down
the attic stairs on a keg, plunging headfirst through the
kitchen door. Small John had lain so still she thought him
dead. No, not Jane.

"Curt? Wilson?"

Pa looked troubled. "I kinda figure on keepin' the boys
home today, Ma. I need 'em at the wall."

"Maybe we'd better send Cuff. He'd show him the way,
for certain sure." Hiram grinned and stood up. Blue-eyed,
strong, stocky, and fifteen, he was confident in his authority as head of the family. "Let me whisk him down, Pa!"

"Need you most of all," said Chauncey Burroughs
slowly.

There was no one who could build a wall like Hi, with
his clever, capable hands. He would select a stone carefully from the long windrow, a pile of stones dumped off

the stone boat, which the oxen, Brock and Bright, had drawn up. He would ease it in with just the right pressure, at just the right angle. He built a wall broad at the base and slowly tapering to the top, smooth and neat on the front side, rough and rugged at the back, and when it was done no storm or frost could undermine it. Even he, Chauncey, couldn't do better, though he had taught the boy himself.

"Come on, feller, let's go! Here's a piece of slate pencil for you."

"Drink up your milk first, Johnny," his mother intervened. But the small boy frowned and pushed back his cup. Wasn't he grown up now? *Milk* indeed!

"Here's a slate, too," cried Olly Ann, throwing a badly cracked one down on the table before she rushed away.

Broken slate pencil and slate—small Johnny grabbed them happily, his sign and seal of office, his proof of manhood.

But if Hiram counted on whisking Johnny to school, he was sadly mistaken. On a wonderful fresh morning in May, alive with entrancing sights and sounds and smells, the little fellow was very much engaged. In the first place, his new cowhides hurt. They weren't so nice to rush in. If he just let Hi get far enough ahead, could he hide behind this wall and take 'em off? It was almost two miles to the stone school at the crossroads, down the rough, winding Hardscrabble Road.

Slowly past a wet place in the woods now, where the spring water still stood gleaming silver between the tree trunks. Hark, what was that—that strange, eerie music like

the tinkling of a thousand chiming little bells? He'd heard
it before, of course, but what made it? Perhaps he'd better
go to see . . .

"Johnny, for the love of Pete, come out o' that wet
place. You'll spile your suit and then won't Ma lick you!
Jumping Jehoshaphat! Sit down this minute and put on
your shoes."

Poor Hiram! The progress was slow and painful. Every
toadstool seemed to entrance small John, even the skunk
cabbages must be inspected. And as for the few farmhouses . . . there he stopped long to look . . . and
look . . .

At last Hiram tossed Johnny up to his shoulder in despair, and trotted swiftly the rest of the way, while the
"ep-lets" jumped and the broken slate, held staunchly by
its red string, slapped against his side. Setting his little
brother down before the teacher at last, he pulled politely
at a dangling copper lock of hair and bobbed his head.

"New pupil for you, Ma'am," he said.

The teacher was young and pretty, chosen for the summer at very low wages, because most of the children would
be kept at home. Johnny eyed her a trifle fearfully with
wide-set, brave blue eyes. He rubbed the end of one both-
ersome cowhide over the other and waited, while a funny
shiver went down his spine. Behind him the other children
tittered, but Hiram patted him reassuringly on the shoulder
as he turned away.

"Why, Johnny . . . isn't it . . . little Johnny Burris?
I'm glad to see you. Your first day at school, and you have
a slate and pencil all ready! Can you write A on your
slate, dear? Do you know A?"

She stooped down and caught his hands and gave them a friendly squeeze. She was nice, Johnny thought. Her nose wiggled a little, like a rabbit's.

"I know A," he proclaimed loudly.

Now she showed him where to sit, on a wall bench that ran along the side of the large, square room. The older children were in the middle, the little fellows at the sides. He climbed up and settled down on it, but his legs had to dangle. There wasn't any place for his feet! The stones in the wall behind him, uncovered by plaster or boards, stuck in his back and hurt. Beside him he saw a small, slender boy with big brown eyes, sitting very still. He didn't have a slate!

"Johnny Burris, this is Hen Meeker," the teacher said.

Slowly the minutes dragged. Minutes? They were hours and hours and hours. He tried writing A and A and A over and over on his slate. School wasn't much fun after all. Nothing happened. Even the pretty lady seemed to have forgotten him. Now and then some of the children marched up to the teacher to say queer words out of books they held in front of them. Jane stuck her tongue out at him, as she clumped noisily by.

At last, stiff and weary from his uncomfortable sitting, small Johnny slid off his bench and began to play in the sand of the floor. This would be better! This wasn't so bad now. Sitting on the ground eased the ache in his legs.

But now the teacher noticed him. Quickly she came to his side and thrust him back on the bench again. "Good boys sit still and keep quiet," she said.

No, it wasn't any fun! Johnny was tired of A's. He was tired of the straining wiggle in his legs, of the pain in his head, of the empty place in his tummy where the milk should have been! He wanted to go home—to play with Cuff, or splash in the brook, or look for red newts under the brown leaves of the woods.

Now he amused himself making his queerest faces at the other children, but they paid no attention at all. "Good boys sit still and keep quiet." He tried to watch a fly buzzing up and down the dim, opposite window. Bee, or fly, he wondered. Bee or fly, fly or bee, bee or . . . or . . . fly . . . or . . . Anyway, he wants to get out and so do I!

Someway the bee and the fly, the mumble of the reciting children, the pain in his legs and the ache in his head, all became part of a tide that was flowing over him, pressing in upon him. Round and round went his head. He tried to keep it straight, but he couldn't. Round and round and round. His tummy seemed to stand up and turn over. There was a sharp, sudden hurt somewhere. Then little Johnny Burroughs entered into a deep blackness and a cracked slate with a dangling red string lay on the sanded floor of the Hardscrabble School.

It was Saturday and Ma was getting ready to bake. All night long the yeasty dough had been rising in a big round pan on the hearth, bubbling and rising under its homespun blanket, as if it had a life of its own. Now it must be kneaded into loaves and poked into the high brick oven beside the fireplace. Ma gasped a little and her face grew red, as she opened the pine door and thrust in a hand to test the heat.

Not hot enough! Not hot enough yet. "More wood, boys, hurry! Curt, Wilson, run to the woodpile for some yaller birch. Quick, flashy wood—that's what I want. You, Johnny, go too." Her eyes lighted on the little fellow quietly watching beside her. "You got no call to be lazy!"

It was then that Bridget, the hired girl, came in, carrying a load of pine. She was tall and stalwart, broad of shoulder and thigh, and she carried the heavy knots with practiced ease. On top of the uppermost lay a strange burden, a lovely bit of black and scarlet, stretched out on the brown pine like a brilliant, crumpled flag.

"See what I found, Ma'am! Poor thing! Must have hit the wood an' broke its neck!"

In spite of her hurry, in spite of her need to have the baking come right, Amy Kelly turned and looked down at the dead tanager on the log with concern in her eyes. She touched the gay plumage and smoothed it gently. How bright and lovely it was, its colors still unfaded, glowing like a jewel in the drab and homely kitchen!

"Ma, why's it so still?"

"It's dead, Johnny."

"Couldn't it eat somethin'?"

"No." And she added slowly, "Shame that a pretty thing like this wouldn't be riding the wind and singing in the forest. But it can't do that no more."

Chauncey Burroughs rushed across the room to claim his pipe, which he had hidden in plain sight on the mantel. He filled it with tobacco from his homemade pigskin pouch, and tamped it down tight with one horny thumb. Then he stamped to the door, shouting back over one shoulder, "Mooning over a dead bird! The silliness of it! Throw it in the fire, Amy, and have done with it. There's a hundred more every minute."

"Not a hundred of these," said his wife gently. "Prettier than a bluebird, even. Don't know that I ever see one before." She sighed, as she saw the reflection of Pa's scorn in Wilson's sneering look, and the mockery in Curt's eyes.

"Riding the wind and singing in the forest." The words made a lovely refrain in Johnny's mind. At the same time there was a strange hurt in his heart. A mist came before his eyes, through which his mother's face swam curiously.

Amy Burroughs glanced down at the little boy, noting his distress, his quick human response. There's more *understanding* in him than in all others of this house, man or child, she thought, and turned competently back to her work.

For a few days after the accident Johnny was kept at home, till the bad cut on his forehead was better and the wound to his spirit healing, too. Then he trudged back to school with the older children, a long way for his short fat legs and for the small feet which wouldn't stay in shoes. Quite happily now he scuffed the rose-brown dirt of the Hardscrabble Road, and swung his new slate high in air.

If Johnny was learning lessons, the teacher learned something too. Young, and not too far from childhood herself, she soon felt fond of the very little boy with the eager blue-gray eyes, who gave the answers so fast. And when, wriggling and overweary from his high, stiff bench, he slipped to the floor, she let him stay there, playing quietly in the sand.

It was the first hot day of spring. The children grew restless and fretful. The eyes of the older boys strayed to the open window, while thoughts of Montgomery Hollow and Rose Brook rippled through their minds like the cool, silver-brown water flowing over stones. The heat, the urgency, the very breath of spring seemed to enter the cramped schoolroom.

There was a sound at the door and the teacher glanced up, irritated, but the visiting trustee who entered paid no attention to her frown. With his firm farmer's stride he marched the length of the room and, parting his coattails neatly, seated himself in the only chair.

"Good morning, children."

Stony-eyed and silent, the roomful of youngsters looked back at him, with only an indistinct murmur from one obliging older girl.

"Children, children!" The teacher rapped sharply on her pine desk with the pointer which lined out the lessons. "Rise when you are spoken to and bow politely! Come, come, where are your manners?"

There came a great shuffling, twisting, wriggling, dropping of books, smothered guffaws. The children struggled to their feet.

"What would you like to hear, Mr. Meeker? A recitation?"

It was almost time to dismiss school. Surely this couldn't last long? But the visiting judge seemed to be in no hurry, no hurry at all.

"The little fellows, how're they doin'? As the twig is bent, you know . . . very important, very important! My son there, what's he a-larnin'?"

He pointed with pride to small Hen Meeker, who sat beside Johnny, looking back at his father with big, frightened eyes. There was a sharp rap on the desk. "First class, come up!" The youngest of all shuffled forward and stood in a frigid row. Held open before them, the dull pages of Cobb's First Reader waited to catch the ignorant and unwary.

"Hen Meeker, what's this?" The teacher's pointer sought out the perpendicular row of squiggles. "Answer, please."

"A . . . I guess."

"Don't you know?"

"Yep."

"And this?"

"C."

"And this?"

There was a long silence, a hanging head, a toe inspected carefully. "Don't know."

"You don't know this, Hen Meeker? You knew it yesterday."

"Don't know now."

The teacher's face grew red. The damp curls about her forehead quivered, the pointer shook. "I'm ashamed, children, I'm really ashamed!" Then as her eyes lighted on Johnny's eager face, she cried, "Johnny Burris'll know, and he's younger than you, Hen. Come forward, Johnny Burris! What's this letter, Johnny?"

"E."

"And this?"

"F."

"And this?"

"W."

"And this?"

So on and on to glory and success—to the teacher's favor, and his own new sense of power. And wasn't Mr. Meeker ashamed of poor ol' Hen? Though Johnny was very young, perhaps the youngest pupil in the little stone Hardscrabble School, he quickly learned that special joy and privilege, the pride and glow of achievement, could come from mastering the pages of the dullest-looking book.

The way back to the farm was long and tiresome after the hard hours shut indoors. If only Olly Ann and Jane would quit yellin' at him. "Come along, Johnny, hurry up, Johnny!" He heard 'em the first time. Well, let 'em get ahead. Didn't he know the way home by now?

Here was that marshy place where the water looked so inviting and where the air seemed alive with a queer shrill music. What made that sound? This time he was going to find out.

He plunged into the marsh, first laying his book and slate down carefully by the roadside. The water wasn't deep, just over his feet. It was a lovely dim, cool world, with the skunk cabbages like green marching soldiers. The thick smell of rotting logs, wet mosses, fungi. A bright orange toadstool stood just before him. What made that constant silvery noise? Soon he would learn, yes, soon he would find out.

Johnny squatted carefully on a hummock of matted grasses. Quietly, very quietly, he settled down to wait. And now the world about which he was so curious ac-

cepted him as a part of itself. From the other end of the
marsh came a soft splashing. From the thicket a yellow-
throat called, "Witchery, witchery, witchery," and up the
quivering cattail, on which Johnny's hand rested, climbed
a mottled brown-gold frog with bulging eyes.

So tiny he was that at first Johnny could not believe in
him. Was he real at all? But he watched him carefully,
hardly daring to breathe, hardly to turn his head. Up, up
the reed the little fellow climbed, one webbed foot over
the other, as a boy might climb a rope. Small—small as a
cricket almost—but clever as a monkey. His eyes were like
round shoe buttons, only they weren't black. In the middle
of each of them was a spot of gold.

Johnny moved one hand up softly and held the reed just
above the tiny frog's head. Since this new brown fungus
was part of his line of march, the peeper accepted it, and
soon Johnny felt the cool, slippery body sliding across his
hand. And now—magic—the little yellowish throat went in
and out, in and out. Content and unafraid, the peeper squatted there, piping his eerie call from Johnny's hand.

So that was it—a frog, no bigger than a minute, made the
strange music that had called him there. *Frogs!* Fascinated,
thrilled with the joy of discovery, the small boy waited,
absolutely still, while all around him, from other reeds and
jutting logs and grasses, shrilled and swelled the deafening
chorus, the wild, urgent, rhythmic music of spring.

Long after Olly Ann and Jane got home, Johnny came
straggling in, wet, bedraggled—and happy. On his face was
a look of secret excitement.

"Where you been, Johnny?" cried his mother anxiously. No, she wouldn't scold him now about his suit.

"Nowhere," said Johnny.

"But what have you been doing, dear? What kept you so long? Why are you so wet?"

Johnny looked up at her. He started to speak, but the words seemed to stumble and stop.

"I don't know, Ma. Nothin', I guess . . . nothin' at all, I guess."

Chapter 3

IT WAS HOT AS JOHN PANTED UP THE HILL PAST THE BEECH trees to call the cows, old Cuff going on before, intent on the errand. Hot! His new flax shirt, not quite broken in, pricked and tortured his skin. John pulled at it and unbuttoned the front, letting the breeze have its way.

He stood in the barway and called, "Co' boss! Co' boss! Co' boss," cupping his slim, brown hands. With no indecent haste the cows ambled forward, each one different from the others, each one a personality, aloof and proud.

"Hi, Whitefoot! Hi, Lophorn! Hi, Muley!" He slapped at the reddish-brown flank of old Brockleface, as she brought up the rear, and laughed when Cuff nipped at her heels to make her jump.

Cuff was taking over now, a flashing streak of gold rounding up the herd. He would march them proudly home, and not too fast. Surely, John thought, he might snatch a moment of freedom.

He ran across the pasture, faster than Cuff himself, a slender, strong little figure, with shirt streaming. There, at the eastward end, towered a boulder of sandstone, which some glacier had left behind eons ago. He climbed expertly, bare hands and feet against red-gray stone, and settled down in triumph at the top. Though he was alone, he drew himself up proudly, lips pursed, arms folded across his chest.

I'm King of the Castle!

If the other boys came by, they would push him off, and what a wrestling match there'd be! But now was peace. And now was a moment to draw one's breath and think one's own thoughts.

He looked down, down, across the wide land below him. Behind him towered Old Clump, and the setting sun threw the shadow of the mountain on the blue, gleaming ridges across the valley. In the distance a vesper sparrow called, three times repeating its clear, lovely strain.

King of the Castle! Well, he would be! Someday he'd come back in a carriage from far away, driving behind black, high-stepping horses. He'd bring his mother gleaming jewels and lovely clothes—blue and silver and red maybe. He'd tell his father to buy all this land. Himself, he'd be great, and very, very rich. Yes, he'd show them!

His hand slid up to the tousled, unkempt mat on top of his head. He fingered the two bumps of his forehead thoughtfully. Hadn't that funny man in the celluloid collar who stopped in at the farm the other day said that his bumps foretold greatness?

Slowly the black shadow of Old Clump crept further and further across the land below him. Hacks Flats, a clearing high on the shoulder of the opposite mountain, caught the last rays of the sun and gleamed like some magic place. Baldy, to the south, retreated into a purple mist. Still John sat on . . . brooding . . . dreaming . . . shivering a little from the rising chill. His first elation had given way to wistfulness.

Greatness! There was a tightness in his throat and a queer heaviness in his chest as he slid down the rock. Then suddenly he laughed. Here was old Cuff, wagging his tail and looking up at him with wide-open mouth and hopeful eyes.

"Come to round me up, old fellow?"

The distant supper bell rang briskly, as he dashed off toward home.

A warm fair Saturday in early June, the sky a blue bowl turned upside down. Amy Kelly looked wistfully out the window and sighed. All day long she had stuck to her indoor tasks, as always—the cleaning, the mending, the beds, the baking, forty milk pans to set and skim, slipping the thick, yellow cream deftly into the cream jar, and then that end of weaving to finish. The clack of the shuttle had made her head ache. Soon, at the afternoon's end, there would be forty more pans to skim.

"Johnny, want to go berrying?"

Johnny, quiet at the kitchen table, was playing a game with himself. Before him lay the dull pages of brown old Cobb's Reader, but they weren't so dull if you fooled with them a little. Look at page ten. Cover it up quickly! See if you can remember all the words. See if you can spell them. Then check at the end. Did you have them right?

Yes, it was even fun, and maybe Jay Gould better look to his place in line at the next spelling bee!

"Sure, Ma. C'm on—let's go!"

They started out together, Amy Kelly covering the fields with her long, easy, swinging stride, and Johnny trotting like a brisk terrier behind her, clanking his pail and whistling. As if in accompaniment, up from the meadows came the gay, bubbling song of the bobolinks.

"Where do we go?" Johnny would know the answer. Of all her children he was the best picker, and he always knew where the biggest berries grew. Partly greed, she thought, smiling to herself, but mostly that he stopped to *look* at things.

"Blackberries biggest down in the ol' bark-peeling. Huckleberries goin' to be best way up top Old Clump."

They went down into the deep valley below the farmhouse, into that strange abandoned place where the hand of man had long ago wrought devastation, but the kindly hand of nature had hidden its trace. Here great rotting logs lay covered with mosses, ferns, and briars, and the scraggly blackberry vines grew thick. Once a virgin forest of hemlocks had stood here, but the tanneries, which needed bark, had sent in hordes of men to cut and strip and waste them. Little but berries were left where the great trees had towered.

Amy Kelly and John turned quickly to their picking, and the first scattering berries pinged into the pails. Suddenly John stopped and lifted his hand. "Partridge!" he said, as his sharp ears caught a distant steady drumming. His mother smiled. For a long moment her hands grew quiet. She lifted her face gratefully and heard, beside the partridge whir-r-r, the long sweeping rush of sound which the wind made as it blew over the miles of forest. Good to be away from the house. Good to hear the music of the wind!

At the edge of evening, they climbed happily back across the meadows, turned into "Hiram's path," then crossed the road to the familiar farmyard. Even before they climbed the stone steps to the door, rough, rasping voices drifted clearly out to them.

Who was there? And who was quarreling? Pa, certainly . . . but who else?

Between the two men seated at the kitchen table lay the big family Bible, in which Chauncey Burroughs had duly recorded the names and births of all his children, but now he was using it for a pounding board, hitting it hard with one clenched fist.

"I tell 'ee, Scudder," he said, " 'tis writ down here, 'Forgive your enemies'!"

"An' I tell you, Chauncey, the Good Book says right here, 'An eye fer an eye, an' a tooth fer a tooth'!"

Yes, they were throwing texts at each other, John thought, much as he and the other fellows sometimes threw stones, but at the sight of Amy Kelly the contest seemed to end.

"Must be gittin' along," Deacon Scudder cried, rising stiffly and shaking one leg a little. "Glad to see you, Ma'am. Full load o' berries you got there. Wisht I could sample one of them pies! Which boy o' yourn is this? John, ain't it?

Don't favor the others none. Don't favor you, Chauncey, one slightest bit. This one's *different*. Sure he belongs in your family?"

He guffawed roughly and tried to catch Johnny's ear while he dodged aside, hating the old man on sight. So he was different, was he? And now Pa answered. "Yep. Don't look a Burroughs, nor act a Burroughs. Let th' Muley cow git in th' corn last week, while he was a-settin' and a-loafin' up on a rock—I seed him—too lazy to drive her home!"

"Chauncey!" Amy Kelly's eyes blazed suddenly. Her voice shook with anger, though she tried to steady it. "You got no call to talk down your own son!" Putting out her hand, she took away the pail which John still held, and swept him quickly into the warm hollow of her arm.

"This boy favors th' Kellys," she said, "and 'tis no disgrace to him either. Blue-eyed like my father, small and quick like him . . ." Nor did she fail to note the darkness which had displaced the joy on John's brooding face.

Different. For days afterwards the word kept coming back to him. Why did it sting and hurt him? Why did he care? "This one don't belong." Was there something wrong with him? Was he really queer? But anyway, Ma understood.

Another year, another spring.

Even before he climbed out of bed Johnny knew by the wiggle in his toes that it was fishing weather. What else should one plan on a bright morning in May when the pink sunrise light stood in the window? He slid into his old blue pants and rolled them to the knees, choosing his smoothest shirt, well broken in. Fishing! The trout would be hungry after their long winter fast, jumping for the fly with a mighty strike or gobbling up the worm and running with it.

He hurried downstairs and scrunched down behind Hiram, as he slid his legs under the unpainted kitchen table. Maybe Pa wouldn't notice him much. If he did, there'd be some new chore, for sure. Manure spreading in the fields, or barn cleaning, or the usual spring wall building would begin, and he'd have to fetch and carry stones. Too early to plow, and they'd finished the sap boiling. But *that* was fun, of course!

He thought with pride of his own ten small cakes of maple sugar stored in the pantry. Hadn't he tapped his tree and boiled down the sap himself? They were the whitest of all. He'd take them down to Roxbury Village and sell them, but not today. Today was for fishing.

Olly Ann was having an "argifying" with Curtis. There were tears in her dark eyes and her pretty face was all screwed up. If she'd been Wilson, Curt would have tackled her; at least, he could scowl and stick out his tongue.

"Nasty little sneak," Olly said with icy distinctness, but Pa brought his fist down on the table and made the dishes jump. Cuff added to the uproar with violent barking.

"By Phagus!" Pa shouted. "It's peace and quiet I ask for at my own board!"

Johnny wolfed his sticky Scotch oatmeal, which he hated, then reached for the reward of pie. Yes, better slip out quietly while Olly Ann was wailing and Pa was making her worse by roaring at her. He glanced at his mother, who was calmly feeding the baby at the other end of the long table. If *she* noticed him, she'd most likely tell him to stay and help with candle dipping. They were almost out of candles, he knew. The long winter evenings had used them up like nobody's business, and she'd just said yesterday they'd have to see to boiling up the tallow. Ugh! Nasty, stinking tallow! Yes, he'd just take his chance while Pa was off guard.

Out behind the barn, in the deep muck at the edge of the manure pile, the angleworms were fat and frequent. He dug them with vim, slipping the juiciest into his tin box along with a sprinkling of earth, and he added plenty of air holes to keep them happy. The battered gray creel, and the pole of striped "whistle wood" over his shoulder, he was off and away. Even old Cuff, the archdetective, hadn't noticed him.

He knew where he was going—for Granther Kelly. Where else? For that young-old boy who had taught him almost all that he knew about fishing, the wily ways of trout and other secrets of the mountain streams. Granther was a bit uncertain in the knees now, his hands were sometimes shaky, but he could still outfish them all.

When he was little, Johnny had just followed along . . . and watched. But now that he was older, Granther had taken him into full partnership and they parceled out the stream between them. "You take Long Reach, Johnny. I'll snake 'em out from that pool below th' alders!"

What flies Granther could make! How deftly and lightly he cast them! A bit of down from a bird's nest, a bit of gold from a flicker's feather, a raveling of red calico, which Granny didn't miss, all bound skillfully together with thin, brown wood fiber into the gayest lure a trout ever snapped at. His line was of horsehair, braided to a fine strength.

"Now, Johnny, now—cast in here on th' deep side o' thet big rock. Keerful, boy, don't let your shadder fall on th' stream! 'Twill warn the trout!"

Johnny hurried up the hill past the pennyroyal rock, then across the mountain pastures, green in their winter rye, toward the old Rundle place. Granny and Granther had moved recently into a little unpainted house on the eastern boundary, to be closer to the home farm.

As he neared the ramshackle porch and started to climb the gray-brown steps, eagerness changed to amazement and joy to wonder. Low, but clear and vibrant, two men's voices drifted out to him, one the deep rumble of a voice he had never heard before, the other unmistakably Granther's. But it was Granther speaking in tongues of fire, excited and intense. Why! Was he praying?

"And grant this poor fugitive thy protection, O Lord! Grant, in thy unspeakable mercy, that he reach the Promised Land in safety."

Hesitatingly, softly and slowly, Johnny pushed open the door. There at the fireplace stood his big, capable Granny, red-faced from the heat of the burning wood. She turned toward him, laying a warning finger on her lips. Beside the bed in the corner Granther was kneeling with hands agonizingly upraised, clasped so tightly together that the knuckles showed white. He wore his old blue army coat and his worn red boots stretched out behind him. Beside him another man knelt, tall and slender and stooped, and as Johnny stared at him, he saw with surprise how white his hair was against the brown darkness of his face.

The Negro sat back on his haunches, then climbed to his feet a trifle stiffly. Granther stood up, too, slowly and breathing hard. He turned, as he did so, to discover his grandson.

"Wal, if 'tain't Johnny come to go fishin'!" he cried, forgetting his Bible English and lapsing into the warm, familiar phrase. "Johnny, I got more important work fer you!" To the colored man he said, "You kin trust my grandson. There's nary a hole or cranny o' this Catskill country he don't know. Johnny, take this friend o' mine up to the ledges on the mountain, to the ones with the cave, where you find th' phoebes' nests."

"Yes, sir!"

"An' don't loiter none, an' don't talk to no one. This be a matter of life or death fer him." He jerked a thumb toward the patiently waiting Negro. "Take the woods trail fer speed, then cut free. He kin hole up on Clump safely till the star shines tonight."

"Granther, what star?"

It was not his grandfather, but the fugitive, who answered. "The North Star, my boy! *My* star. The one the Lord stood in th' sky like a lamp to my feet so hit kin show me th' way to freedom."

Boy though he was, Johnny was stirred by a queer thrill

of compassion. He noticed how frail the old man seemed, how anxiously he glanced around the yard as they went out, how carefully he scanned the pasture in front, the edge of the woods; even, it seemed, the hills.

With all the expertness at his command, Johnny hurried along the trail through the hemlocks, then on to the beech woods where the great gray trunks stood guard. He hardly dared turn to see whether the mysterious stranger was behind him and though he strained his ears to listen, only the drumming of a redhead or the soft sigh of the wind seemed to answer him.

To his dismay, as he started up a little rise of ground, he saw a familiar form striding toward him down the narrow path.

"Mornin', Mr. Bartram!" Surely, even though it was forbidden, he must speak to this well-known neighbor who was meeting him face to face.

"Why ain't you in school, Johnny?"

"See what I'm carrying, Mr. Bartram?"

"Oh, oh—fish, eh? Wal, good luck anyhow! My gal will be ahead o' you in spellin' by tomorrow."

Johnny grinned and hurried on. "I'll ketch up with her, Mr. Bartram."

Would the Negro be seen? Beads of heat stood out on Johnny's forehead; he licked his lips nervously. He had been trusted with a serious mission. Was he failing in it? Or had his brief exchange with the farmer given the old fugitive time to hide? Just once he glanced back cautiously over his shoulder.

Hi Bartram was already lost in the distant woods; only

the fresh golden green of the May forest stood behind him, through which the trail ran, a thin, brown, sun-flecked line. At first he stood still, listening; then, very softly, he ventured a low whistle. No answer.

For ages, it seemed, he waited. Then, striking the flat of his hand across his mouth, he gave a wild Indian call. Enough to wake the dead and make anyone know that he was being summoned. If Bartram heard it, far off as he was now, he would think that Johnny was just having fun. Surely the Negro would come?

No answer except for the soft forest voices, the whistle of an inquisitive chickadee.

At last Johnny hotfooted it back down the trail to burst breathless and almost sobbing through the familiar door.

"Johnny, what's wrong, dear?" Granny pushed back the straggling locks of chestnut hair that always got in his eyes, and patted one damp shoulder. But Granther knew.

"So you lost th' feller?"

"Hi Bartram come, Granther. I had to answer him. And then . . . and then . . . the man was gone . . . just nowhere . . . gone!"

"Um," said Granther. "Don't worry, son. You done th' best you could. These fugitive fellers is wary as foxes an' scary as rabbits. He's found his own hide-out, never fear. I put him up fer one night, but I couldn't hold him. If you hadn't talked to Farmer Bartram, he might 'ave seen th' feller an' given him up. He's all fer law an' order, Brother Bartram is. Me, I kinda figure on mercy. Zuckers! What's that rod fer, Johnny? Come on, let's go trouting down in th' hemlocks."

For years this strange episode of his youth stayed in John Burroughs' mind. Later, when the great war between the states broke out in all its demonic fury, though his mother and father were Copperheads—Northerners who sympathized with the South—he himself, with passionate conviction, stood for Abe Lincoln and the cause of the slaves. For from Granther Kelly, who had fought with Washington and known the cruel rigors of Valley Forge, Johnny Burroughs learned many things. One of them was the value of freedom.

Chapter 4

Granther and Johnny fished on and on. The day seemed to be without beginning and without end, with a kind of timeless passing which was like the flowing of the mountain stream they followed. When the sun was high and they grew hungry, squatting on the bank they built a fire and cooked the smallest of the trout they had caught. Cleaned and impaled on a stick, these toasted to a delicious brown, with all the flavor of sun and stream and fire intact at their heart.

But the light faded at last and Granther cocked a knowing eye at the shadows. "Best be gittin' home, Johnny. Most six o'clock, I reckon."

Johnny sighed. "Hate to leave now. It's the best fishing time."

"Yep, I know! But the dark's fishin' fer us, and I got no aim to be caught on th' trail without th' light."

Johnny shivered suddenly, realizing at once the older man's wisdom and fear. No, Granther, who believed in spooks and goblins and puckhas, Granther who was Irish to the core, wouldn't wish to be caught by the forest darkness. Nor, for that matter, would he! Impulsively he seized his grandfather's hand. "Come home with me, Granther, come spend the night. Mom would like it fine."

A broad, cheerful grin greeted his invitation. Slowly the old man began to collect his duffel—the beech rod, the flies, the line, the long row of trout expertly strung on a willow shoot, and Johnny sorted out his own biggest trout to a place on top in the gray creel, moistening them lovingly with wet moss to keep them cool and fresh.

"C'm on, then! Must stop by and tell Granny."

Grandmother Kelly was already cooking supper. She snorted at the offer of fish. "Ain't got no fat to cook 'em in, nor wood to spare, fer that matter. Wood box empty, Pa! If you're goin' to Amy's, give her my love an' come back early. Kitchen garden must git dug! And take off those wet boots when you git thar."

"Yes, Ma, surely—surely."

Granther seized his old blue army coat and fled with Johnny. But at his daughter's house he was given a riotous welcome. Even before they had climbed the stone work in front, the children seemed to sense his coming.

The open door, with Amy Kelly smiling and waving. Small Abigail, with flying yellow braids, skipping down the steps to meet him. Now Hiram slapping him on the back, while Curt and Wilson yanked his coattails and Olly Ann smacked him on one ear. And Cuff, the bobtailed mastiff, managed in the general fracas to land one good lick upon his chin.

"Wal, wal, zounds and zuckers!" cried Granther, pretending distress, but hugely and highly delighted. He seemed to gather them all into the circle of his two long arms and sweep them so into the front door before him.

When supper was over and the flames were licking their way bravely up the chimney, while the shadows danced over the dark red walls of the kitchen, and the May chill caught at their backs, now came the time which the children loved—and dreaded.

"Granther, a story—a story!" they clamored, and Grandfather smiled his long, slow, crooked smile.

Amy Kelly reached for her basket of socks to mend, and shoved herself along the settle to a place where the firelight could help, for the one tallow dip they allowed themselves would be saved till the evening's end.

Chauncey Burroughs' sandy freckled face grew solemn. He stooped to empty his pipe on the hearth, then poked and pummeled in the fresh tobacco. Hiram started to mend a bit of harness, Curtis to whittle out some needed shingles, but Johnny sat rapt and silent, waiting for the stories to begin.

"Wal, when I was a boy, I was standin' on a hill in Ireland. I was standin' in the middle of a field on the side o' old Knock Bhuv, and the mist come blowin' and driftin' by in great white sheets; 'twas driftin' in my face. All unbeknownst to myself, belike, I had me hand on the limb of a wild thorn tree. 'Twas the edge of evening and the darkness was comin' fast, and what with the mist and the dark I was bemused entirely. 'Twas then I was for hearin' a great and horrible neigh—two awful glaring eyes burned out o' the driftin' mist. Zounds! A great black horse, a-comin' at me fast . . ."

"The Puckha!" shrieked small Eden, who had heard the story before.

"The Puckha!" echoed Abigail, burying her yellow head in Johnny's lap.

Protectively John put his hand down on the little girl's shaking braids. Though he pretended unconcern, he felt none too steady himself.

"With a whoosht and a roar and the breath of a thousand winds, the great black horse had me swept upon his back. High over hill an' dale, high over lake an' mountain he flew, and me whimperin' and holdin' to his mane, and begging to be put down for the dear love of Heaven. But divil a bit would he slacken for all that—till at last we come to the sea. And it roarin' and foamin' and dashin' upon the rocks and I thinkin' at any minute to be drowned in the waves.

" 'Twas then there come a terrible wailin' like the warning call of the banshees, together with a blinding flash of light . . . and I felt meself fallin'—down, down, down—while the great black horse, like a bit o' bog mist, disappeared entirely.

"When I come to meself again, I was lyin' all alone on a bleak an' stony hillside, with no sense of where, and even less of whither . . ."

"But Granther, how did you ever get home?"

"Oh, the weary walkin' and oh, the weary askin' . . ."

Now it was the tale of the graveyard "just the other night," round the bend in the road where the stones stood white and still.

"Suddenlike I saw a light, as big as a millstone . . .

now 'twas big as a washtub. Creation to cats! I started to run, but the light come rollin' after me."

Poor Johnny! When he crawled slowly up to bed that night, all the shadows seemed to follow him. Every creak of the stair boards brought a shiver of fright. For the Irish inheritance, which gave him courage and imagination, gave him also an undue burden of fear. He was too old to be afraid of the dark; he knew it was childish and unreal. He knew, too, that his grandfather had never been in Ireland. But all the primitive world of Granther Kelly, all the spooks and will-o'-the-wisps and puckhas seemed to come and capture him again. For Granther Kelly, whom he loved, believed it all himself.

Later, when the children were in bed, their mother came up the stairs to say good night. Feeling that they had really had too much, she stooped over Olly Ann and Jane and little Abigail with special tenderness, tucking the blue homespun "kiverlid" in carefully around them. Then she came across the hall to see Wilson, Curtis, and John. They lay huddled together in one big four-poster, where Johnny already had the covers over his head, though he was far from sleeping.

Amy Kelly tweaked down the smothering comfortable, giving one lock of hair a sudden tug and smiling down at him. "Better come up fer air, Johnny," she said.

As she stood in the door a moment, glancing back at the boys, Johnny did a strange thing. *Look at her*, he said to himself. Some day she won't be here. Look at her hard— and *remember*. And so he studied her as if she were a picture or the page of a book that he must master.

He saw the sturdy, stoutish figure, not over tall. He saw the serene face with its deep, brooding eyes, now half in shadow. The light of the candle struck upwards and outlined the broad, lovely forehead, the little straight nose with its high, strong bridge. The mouth he could not see, but he knew that it stood for kindness.

Shading the tallow dip with a hand against the draught, Amy Kelly turned away.

"Hiram, go hitch up Prince and Pete to th' pleasure wagon!"

Chauncey Burroughs never said please, but as regularly as Sunday rolled round he gave this order to his oldest son, who rose at once to obey it.

Johnny, seated at the drop-leaf cherry table with his head bent over the *Life of Washington*, came back to Roxbury with a start. His father's strident voice could banish the thrills and terrors of Bunker Hill. He knew what was coming next, too—and it came.

"Time to spruce up fer church, Johnny!"

The youngster closed his book with a bang, but the gray-blue eyes met his father's with a quizzical twinkle in their depths. Long ago, as he did his outside chores, he had noted the perfect, golden June day inviting and beckoning. He wasn't tame like Hiram, and that was the cheese of it!

"Pa?"

"Wal?"

"Ain't there a ewe and her lamb missing from the upper pasture?"

"M-m-m-m-m," said the elder Burroughs, shifting his

pipe from one corner of his mouth to the other, then sending the smoke out in forceful puffs. "Did calculate yestiddy they wan't all there."

"And don't all the sheep need salting?"

"Wal—mebbe."

Blue eyes met brown in a long, steady look. Johnny was thinking, Don't send me to be shut up for hours in that stale, old church at Shackville to listen to Elder Hewitt's dull singsong. He's never even interesting unless he comes to Hell fire, and sends the Methodists there, but there isn't enough of that!

There's one thing Johnny's good fer, Chauncey Burroughs thought, and the other boys don't do it as well. He kin find th' lost beasts. Sheep or cow or horse, he seems to sense where they go—an' when found, they foller him. He'll find the ewe. It's my duty to eddicate him in the church, but the sheep do need salting! Boy can't plow or dig or hoe too good. He's no count at loadin' hay. When I send him to cut wood, he sets down behind th' woodpile an' reads. But he do find beasts.

Amy Kelly opened the door from her bedroom to sweep into the kitchen with her full black silk skirts rustling a brave Sunday rustle. Her one good dress, and she was proud of it. She looked beautiful, and important, John thought, and little Abigail capering beside her was sweet as maple sugar in her pink sprigged calico, with sunbonnet to match.

"Coming to church, John?"

"No, Ma. Going to salt th' sheep."

Amy Kelly sighed. If the sigh betokened envy, that she,

too, would have liked a free June day on Old Clump, she gave no further word or sign. But she turned to the other boys with the same question. "Coming to church, Wilson? Curt?"

"No, Ma, we'll help Johnny!"

Standing at the front door, barefooted and free, Johnny gazed down at the three-seater in the road below. It was Pa's one great extravagance, hand made by old Neil Dart and "ironed" at Enderlin's blacksmith shop in the Hollow. Bright and shiny black with yellow wheels, gay and new. Heaven knew what it had cost in their own labor and his mother's toil, or where the money came from to pay for it! Butter money, most likely. If he could ride in it, maybe he would have weakened and gone to church, but there was never room for the "big boys." They had to walk cross-lots to the Old Baptist Meeting House. Pa and Ma and Olly Ann and Jane, Abigail and Eden and the baby Eveline—they seemed to fill it well. Now Hi yielded the reins to Pa, the whip cracked, the harness creaked, Prince and Pete strained forward, they were off and away. The dust of the road rose behind them like puffs from Pa's old pipe.

"C'm on, Johnny, let's go to th' Deacon woods."

This wasn't the right way to reach the sheep, who were just in the opposite direction, but the hours stretched ahead, timeless and beckoning. A whole long day. What couldn't one do, where couldn't one go in a day! Hugging his block of rock salt to his old homespun shirt, he tagged after the older boys.

First they followed the road in front of the house, going Hardscrabble way. Now a sweeping bend and a long hill, to be taken slowly. Here a sharp turn to the east along a thin path, hardly more than a forest trail. To the south, where they could see it through the thinning trees, the land fell away in a steep, rocky ravine, and all the glory of the Catskill country, fold on fold of blue gleaming peaks, seemed to lie beyond. Far, far below to the west they could see their own farm stretched out.

This was the Deacon path, named for old man Scudder, for whom they surely had no love. Didn't he clump up to the church gallery to deal with them if they so much as whispered there during service? As for Johnny, he had a special hate for him ever since that day in the kitchen when the old man told him he "didn't belong!"

The Deacon woods were cool and dim and fragrant, and the towering beech trees looked like old gray elephants with their slaty, wrinkled bark. Johnny loved them. He loved the massive thicket of mountain laurel, rose-colored along the edge of the ravine. He loved the fern smell and the leaf-mold smell, the faint fragrance of maidenhair, and the sudden surprise of a lady-slipper, looking up from the floor of the forest.

Curt and Wilson were doing stunts. First they dared each other to shinny up a straight trunk; then, tired of that, they started to throw knives at it. Johnny, who wasn't allowed to compete, grew weary of watching. He strolled on.

Under a hemlock tree he threw himself on his back and gazed up at the distant pattern of flat, green needles set against a blue sky. Slowly he munched some wintergreen leaves, liking the crisp taste; then he sucked a stick of black birch, smooth and sweet. Peace . . . quiet . . . his own way . . . how could there be a better Sunday?

Down from the patterned blue and green above him came suddenly a strange, buzzing call. Like an insect, yet different from an insect. A bird? But not like any bird he had ever heard. And then a tiny flash of grayish blue shot its irregular way down through the branches. Alert at once, he sat up and tried to follow it with his glance—strained to see, listened intently. Now the buzzing "Wee, wee, wee, weep" seemed far above him; now it came closer, closer, and the source of it for a moment stood clear.

Yes, gray-blue, with a white breast and a throat of inky black. A song that was not a song, from a bird he had never seen before! And now, as it flitted on, he quickly noted the clear white spots upon its wings.

"Curt, Wilson," he called, eager in spite of himself to share his mounting excitement. "Look, look," he yelled, and pointed as they came running. "A new bird! What . . . what's its name?"

"Oh, that!" growled Curt in disgust, turning away. "Thought you'd found something!"

"Just a bluebird, little idiot," sneered Wilson. "You do get het up over nothing!"

"Little idiot." It was always what they thought of him. Why couldn't they care, too? But for once the joy would not leave him, or the excitement die away. This wasn't a bluebird—it couldn't be! He had found a new bird, he knew he had, something he had never seen or known before. There might be more of them. There might be hundreds of birds he didn't know, maybe thousands. It was as

if a door had opened suddenly into a new room of beauty and promise and joy—and he could enter it. He knew, he felt sure, that someday he would *go through the door*.

When Johnny came home that afternoon, the lamb was tight in his arms and the ewe and Cuff were tailing him in solemn procession. Chauncey Burroughs laughed at them, when he saw the little group come into the barnyard, but for once he was pleased.

By Phagus! he thought. Ain't no way o' telling what that boy'll ever come to, but anyway . . . he's mighty good at finding lost beasts.

The weeks after Johnny first saw his new bird, he often hunted for it again. He looked for its nest in the Deacon woods, but in spite of patient trying he never succeeded in finding it. What was it? When would he see it again, or when would other strange birds come his way? These, and many other questions, filled his eager, curious mind.

Over and over he found the nest of a vesper sparrow, laid trustingly on the ground of the open pasture with little more than a thistle or bit of tansy to shelter it. Many a tall stump yielded a bluebird's or a redhead's nest. He loved to smack the stump with his stick to see the anxious woodpecker flutter out. And once he found an ovenbird's home set in the dry leaves of a wooded trail, with its canopy so cunningly arched that the whole was indeed like a small, brown oven. But the little black-throated blue warbler he could not find.

The weeks of summer stretched out—hot, dry, and tiresome, with only the cool, rippling brooks, the deep shade of the forest, the wind off Old Clump to make life bearable. Then came the hardest time of all on the farm—the long thirty days' struggle called haying. Now all hands were needed, every man or boy on the farm, any neighbor who was willing and not too hard-pressed at home, all hired men from miles around who were foot-loose and free. Since the army of men needed food and help, women and girls were busy too. Amy Kelly seemed never to rest from turning out mountains of rye bread, doughnuts, pancakes, johnnycake, countless rounds of pie.

"If 'tweren't fer you, Olly Ann, don't know where I'd be!" she often cried.

The sun scorched down on the hot, aching backs of men, on muscles rippling in burned arms and shoulders, on tall, green grass laid low by the flashing scythes. Acre after acre of mountain meadow must yield to the swinging blades, for winter feed for the cattle was the most important need of all on a big dairy farm.

Johnny at ten was too young and slight to do scything, or so his mother said. Pa sniffed, but yielded to her wish, though he never failed to add, "Johnny'll be no good if you coddle him!" Sometimes he set the lad a brief swath to cut, "just to break him in," and Johnny found himself liking the swing of the blade, the slow rhythm of the mowing.

"Takes skill, not strength, Ma," he told his mother, but still she objected to his joining Curt and Wilson. As it was, he was busy from sunup to sundown, everybody's chore boy, never his own master.

"Fill the water jug, boy!"

"Fetch the lunches, Johnny."

Or some worker slipped his blade from the snath, pushing in an extra one. "My blade's kinda dull. Take it back to th' grindstone, feller!"

When, later, the hay was cured and raking time came, Johnny could work with the men. He liked to wait till the ground was thickly covered with a great pile of hay, then plunge into it with a will. But this habit seemed to annoy his father. If he paused a moment, Pa Burroughs called, "Rake, Johnny! What you waitin' fer?"

"Waitin' till there's more *to* rake."

"You rake what there is."

Now haying time was over, the gathered loads safely stored in the barns. Life turned to its even tempo again, but Johnny still worked in field or stable, all thought of school left far behind in the spring.

Autumn—and a brilliant mantle of rose, scarlet, and gold flung over the hills. Soon this, too, faded till the tall pines, the hemlocks, and the spruces with their spires seemed to become masters of the land, while here and there an oak tree clung to its dried, plum-colored leaves.

Talk at the farm was all of the coming event of the year—the butter trip to Catskill. It would be a long, hard journey—four days in the November chill, seated on the high board beside Pa, while Ma's firkins of butter rode and jounced behind, but how the children hoped and dreamed of going! "Whose turn is it? Take me, Pa, you never take me!"

Hiram had been many times; Curt and Wilson each more than once; Eden was too young. Johnny was sure it was his turn unless—oh, horror of horrors—Pa chose a *gal.* Would Pa think he was strong enough to spell him with the driving, to help move the tubs? With all his heart he longed to go over the mountain for his first glimpse of a wider world. At night he dreamed of it and by day he thought of little else. Hi laughed at him and said he was "all in a pucker."

Then came a morning when, rubbing his eyes sleepily, Johnny went out to the stable in the half-light of early dawn. The cows stood in two long rows; white smoke seemed to come from their nostrils as they stamped and moved in the chill air. Johnny swung his lantern, trying to whistle, and suddenly the shadow of a seated figure leapt like some black demon across the wall.

"Pa . . . here a'ready?"

"Johnny, I don't loiter none when there's work to do."

For a while they sat side by side without further word, and the warm milk squirted into the pails. Then Chauncey Burroughs turned his head toward Johnny and smiled. "Doing pretty good, son. You'll be a milker yet. Done pretty good all summer. Wa'n't bad at rakin'. Like a trip to Catskill next week? Hey?"

The lad's heart seemed to miss a beat; his eyes flashed as he looked at his father. As always, when he was deeply moved, he stammered a little.

"You b-bet I w-w-would, Pa!"

It was pitch-dark, long before dawn, when Prince and Pete pulled out the old lumber wagon, loaded the night before with hundred-pound tubs of butter, yellow as gold. Gold it was to this farm family, who depended hopefully on its sale. Hi held the tin lantern; Curt and Wilson threw in bags of oats for the horses, a box of venison, partridge, and rye bread for Pa and Johnny. Ma and the girls stood shivering in the early morning cold.

Wrapped to the eyebrows in the huge family greatcoat, which trailed about his heels, Johnny climbed gingerly up by feel to the high springboard in front. At the last Ma tried to wind a thick wool tippet about his neck, but once on the seat he pulled it off and threw it behind him. Pa laughed as he caught the gesture and said aloud to no one in particular, "Boy's growin' up. Won't be babied no more!"

To Johnny came a sudden sense of man-to-man comradeship, a feeling of affection for the gruff dad beside him, as they rattled away from farewell calls. Pa had chosen him. He was going away alone with him. Wasn't he 'most a man? Sure, he was!

First north past the "little stone jug" at Hardscrabble, where he had had his early schooling not so long ago; then north again to Grand Gorge. Thick white mists rolled ghostlike in the valleys. Prince and Pete settled down into a rapid jog; their heels beat a sharp staccato on the frozen road.

Now south to Prattsville and east to Windham Mountain. Slowly the horses toiled up the long, winding track, now stopping to rest on a welcome thank-you-marm, now straining patiently forward. Could they, John wondered, endure to reach the top?

Pa broke his silence, and turned to the youngster beside him. "Seems slow to you, don't it, Johnny? But the fust time I come this way 'twas slower yit. Yep, my pa brung me when I was knee-high to a grasshopper, younger'n you be, son. We come by oxcart. Took us more'n a week. Was nothin' else to use then."

"Where was you born, Pa?"

"In a log house, Johnny, and eight others 'sides me. Born close to th' stump I was—you ain't so far from it yourself—an' don't fergit it!"

The sweeping view from Windham Mountain seemed to take John's breath away. All the kingdoms of the earth seemed spread before them—dark, mysterious valleys, peaks purple or snow-capped, shimmering in the winelike winter air. But the Hudson River, toward which they strained, was still far to the east.

It was late when they drove into the inn yard at Cairo, and tavern doors opened to receive them. Welcoming heat. Warm smells of roasts turning before the fire, of stews and hot bread, of simmering toddy or rum punch steaming on the hearth.

"Pork stew an' green tea fer two," Pa bellowed, striding past the bar with never a sideward glance. Johnny followed, his oversized greatcoat sweeping the floor behind him, conscious of leeward snickers as he passed. He found himself wondering why, with all these strange, wonderful, and delicious smells, Pa had to order just what they ate at home!

The sun was already up when Johnny woke the next morning. His father had disappeared. He was quickly worried lest he had delayed the trip or, indeed, lest the trip had continued without him. Why hadn't Pa called? He drew on his leather breeches in haste and pulled the

warm woolen shirt over his head. His mother had loomed
it for him, dyeing it brown with butternut bark. But the
family greatcoat he left behind as he dashed down the
stairs, out into the inn yard. Yep, it was Pa, all right! That
rough, strident voice, that carrot-colored hair under the
fur hat could belong to no one else.

"Boy's a smart one, I tell ye," Pa was saying to a group
of men. "Kin rig up the team as good as me. That's why
I brung him stead o' my hired man . . ."

"Why don't you give us an—er—demonstration, Mr.
Burroughs?" a seedy onlooker questioned in a high, reedy
voice, while the other men laughed.

Were they making fun of Pa? And, horror of horrors,
was Pa bragging about *him?* Johnny turned to make a
bolt for it, but in that split second Chauncey Burroughs
saw him.

"So there ye be, son. Just tellin' these men you're a right
smart helper. Go on into th' stable, will ye, and harness
Prince an' Pete. Drive 'em out yourself. Hurry up now!"

Poor Johnny! Though his ribs seemed knocking together from hunger, his eyes still full of sleep, he tackled
bridle, bit, and snaffle with cold and fumbling fingers.
And when the horses stood with the whiffletree between
them, he climbed to the springboard seat and took up
the reins.

"Giddap! Git on there, Prince!" He slapped at the
broad backs with his reins. The sturdy team jumped forward, the sides of the barn seemed to flash past. Even
as they neared the narrow doorway, Johnny realized
in an instant of fear that they were heading for it at a dangerous slant. Too late he pulled back on the leather, but

no strength of his could stop the forward rush. There came a crash, the sickening sound of splintering wood, as the wheel hub caught the doorjamb in vicious impact. Hanging on desperately, he still held to the reins, while the horses reared and plunged in helpless confusion.

Johnny didn't blame his father for being angry. Again he had failed and embarrassed him, had proved himself the bungler that he always seemed to be. But to ride the long, cold miles in still colder silence was almost more than he could bear. Now and then a farmer met them; once an ox team dragging a sledge full of wood. At noon the stage from Catskill came racketing by, four horses in headlong speed with the coach swaying back and forth like a rocking chair. But Chauncey Burroughs ignored them and held to his sullen quiet.

When they crawled at last over the final high divide of the Catskills and saw the great blue river valley stretching deep down below them, Johnny forgot his woes and cried out in amazement, "Pa, it's the *Hudson*, isn't it?" And Pa broke his frigid silence to answer, "Yep."

A thin line of silver set in a blue land, growing wider and wider, until it seemed to become a turquoise sea on which small white sails drifted back and forth like the wings of strange, new birds.

"Schooners—sailin' down their wares to trade at New York!" Pa said.

Most exciting of all, a long white line of smoke streaming back from what looked like a great gray beetle.

"Day boat fer Albany—thar she goes!"

A *steamer*. It had even made Pa forget his grudge. Someday, John told himself, he would ride on one. Someday he would sail on down to the sea. The hours that followed seemed to the country boy like a series of slides from some wonderful magic lantern. Everything was new, amazing, different. The weighing of the butter, when the heavy firkins were swung onto the weighing platform by block and tackle, not by the straining hand power to which he was used. The argument with old Dowie, the butter buyer, when he accused Pa of mismarking a firkin's weight.

"This here tub's of heavier wood, Burroughs. I kin see it. Ain't so much butter!"

"By cracky," bellowed Pa, "strip it, strip it, I tell 'ee! The naked butter'll tell the truth. Strip it!"

When the big round of butter stood free from its tub upon the scales, Johnny rejoiced to see that Pa had won. For Ma's golden butter weighed just what Pa had said it did.

Then the wharves at Catskill Point by the river's edge, with their wares standing in tumbled piles. Men arguing and haggling. The sweeping flight of great white gulls. All the glory and variety of the passing Hudson. Here Pa bought three hundred herring to salt, and gypsum which would fertilize the fields at home.

Now the stores, and the excitement of purchase—calico for the girls, fancy delaine for Ma. Johnny waited patiently, eying a wool cap trimmed with a band of muskrat fur. When he saw it in Pa's hands, he wondered which of the boys would win it. But when Pa turned and clamped it down suddenly on his own head, he felt as if the ground would give way beneath him.

So Pa wa'n't mad any more. Maybe Pa even liked him.

A great load of grief and self-doubt seemed to roll away.

It was late on the fourth night when Prince and Pete turned into the stable yard at Roxbury. But quickly the old tin lantern and Hiram's shadowy form behind it raced forward to meet them. Now Ma crying, "Well, well! Here at last!" Abigail reaching up to grasp him with a short, hard hug; Cuff giving the queer, ecstatic yelps which were his own special offering, only for Johnny.

Home, with all its warmth and kindliness and cheer; the oneness of the family taking him in.

"What did we make, Pa?" asked Amy Kelly.

"Eighteen and a half cents a pound," said Chauncey Burroughs proudly.

Chapter 5

JOHNNY CAME BACK FROM SCHOOL AND LEAPT UP THE
stairs to his own room, two steps at a time. Off came his
coat, bang went his black oilskin bag on the floor, while his
slate flew through the air to land on the feather bed.

Wonder of wonders! From under his bed, lying along
the floor, two legs in blue "jane" were sticking out. From
deeper in under the bed came a muffled sneeze. Now the
legs wriggled and shook, and inch by inch their owner
emerged, sneezed again, and brushed the woolly dust from
his hair.

"Hi! What in thunder?"

"Didn't mean you to catch me, feller! Didn't mean no
one to know!"

"But what were you doin'?"

"Look under!"

Johnny bent double and peered under the bed. There, in
a shadowy corner against the wall, lay what looked like
a crumpled rug.

"Can't see nothin'."

"It's Ma's old carpetbag; she won't miss it. I've got it
full o' my duffel," Hi added cryptically.

"Whatever for?"

"Because I'm runnin' away."

"Running away!" A thrill of excitement shot down Johnny's spine—a flame of exaltation. Good old quiet hardworking Hi, twenty-three years old and never been in mischief! Good old Hi, planning this revolt . . .

"Yep, I'm goin' West—mebbe meet up with Kennedy."

"To *California?*"

"Yep. Don't I know how to dig? Ain't I strong and well? Can't I find gold as good as the next feller?"

"Oh, Hiram, take me with you!"

"Couldn't do that, boy. Got to inch my way. Sail to New Orleans, then work. Walk a piece, work some more . . . get to Panama, then walk across . . ."

"Oh, Hi, it'd be great."

"Great . . . an' dangerous—yep. No, you stay here, Johnny. Mebbe I'll send fer you. Mebbe we'll prospect together."

"Goin' soon, Hi?"

"Wal, not till after sugarin' is over. Pa'd never make the spiles and drive the gouges without me."

"No, nor carry the iron pots, nor watch the biling."

"Nope. Don't tell, Johnny. I'm countin' on you. *Don't tell.*"

For days Johnny hurried home early, fearing and hoping to find that Hi had gone. Why did he want him away, the brother he loved the best, ten years older, more like a gentler, kinder Pa? It was Hi who had toted him to school when others thought him too little and a nuisance. It was Hi who had made him toys—little men from corncobs, a mill that would really run with water from the brook, that would cut the cucumbers they used for "pretend" logs! Sunup and sundown, Hiram was always working. No one could make ax handles and neck yokes, no one could cut shakes or mend harness or lay up stone walls like Hi. If Pa knew, he would never let him go.

As the days lengthened into weeks, and the crumpled carpetbag gathered dust, Johnny's excitement faded. But one day he cornered Hi and put it to him straight. "Don't believe you're ever goin', Hi!"

"Yep, I be, Johnny."

"This week, maybe?"

"Wal, Pa's fixin' to wall up that west pasture above th' sap bush . . ."

"So you'll stay for that?"

"Reckon I must . . . and there's a square dance in th' Hollow next week. Kinda said I'd call . . ." Hiram's nearsighted, pale-blue eyes grew wistful. "It's harder than I thought to git away!"

"Hard? It's you that make it hard, fixin' to do every-thing anyone says." The younger boy's eyes blazed sud-denly with a flash of excitement, then deepened to a new darkness—strange eyes that could vary in tone and color, Irish eyes, like his mother's. Was there pity in them, pity . . . and a shade of contempt?

"Hiram, if I ever plan to run away, no sap bush or stone wall or square dance'll stop me—and no Pa, neither. I'll just . . . *go*."

"Yep, bet you will, Johnny." Hiram's voice grew sad. "But then, you're *different*."

"Ain't you taking a gal to the dance, Hi?"

"Yep, but you can come along. Sue Ellen likes you. You ain't poison, Johnny."

"No, but he's too young," Amy Kelly cried out in vigorous protest. "Late hours . . . bad company . . ." She laid a hand on Johnny's arm and looked anxiously into his face.

Johnny, who really loved his mother, was aware of the widening gulf between them. For once it was Pa who came to his rescue with a blustering "Nonsense! Boy's got to learn to dance. I knew how at fourteen. So'd you, Amy!"

Amy withdrew her hand, picked up a plate and put it down for no apparent reason, sighed . . . and turned away.

Hiram looked after her understandingly. "Sue Ellen and I'll keep an eye on him, Ma," he said.

The May moon was riding high over sleeping fields and hills when Hiram and Johnny started for the dance. They passed Jane waiting at the door for her swain to come by, and with farewell waves started down West Settlement way along the white, winding road. To the south stood the small graveyard, where crooked stones gleamed faintly in the moonlight. In spite of himself, the old spine-tingling sense of unease and fear came to Johnny as he passed the lonely place—that heritage from Granther, which it was hard to outgrow. He was glad when they turned sharply downhill along the familiar way to school.

Picking up Sue Ellen, they went cross-lots now toward the Hollow, Hi and his girl in front, Johnny tagging tactfully behind. As he followed he could hear the sound of

voices, though not the words, now and then a note from
Hi's jew's-harp, or a gay burst of laughter from Sue
Ellen. The smell of fresh earth relenting under the warmth
of spring brought pleasure to Johnny's country nostrils.
He listened for the faint twitter of a night bird, noted a
dim, passing shape at the edge of the woods. In the moonlight maple buds showed a soft rose color.

Before they reached the old barn dedicated to dances,
a square of light stood out in the distance. There came the
warm throb of dancing feet shaking the boards; nearer
still—the thin squeak of a fiddle, the shout of the caller . . .

The place was alive, John saw, with strong young bodies
moving back and forth, on and around, weaving and re-
weaving into new and intricate patterns of light and color—
vigorous, rhythmic, unrestrained. From under the pounding feet rose a faint dust that misted the high, dim lanterns.

As they stood watching, Hiram turned to Johnny.
"Mighty purty, ain't it?" he said.

Now the music stopped; the patterns fell apart; the
whirling shapes became talking groups or couples drifting
aimlessly, with here or there a boy or girl leaning against a
hand-hewn upright, alone.

"Hi! Here's Hi!" A shout went up from the dancers as
their favorite caller entered the barn, and "Wal, ef 'tain't
Johnny!" came occasionally as a friendly afterthought.
Without a backward glance, Hi left Sue Ellen, mounted
the platform, and greeted the fiddler, who cried, "Here
ye be!" as he grinned and waved his bow.

Hi slouched to the edge of the boards, flexing his knees,
flailing his arms, nonchalant and relaxed. His blond hair
stood up round his head like the stubble of a badly mowed

meadow. He had knotted a gay kerchief about his throat; one hand waved the jew's-harp. Out over the crowd his resonant voice carried with strong, rhythmic stress, set to the sliding, nasal drawl of the perfect caller. Johnny stared in amazement, while the crowd stamped and clapped. This was a new Hiram, electric with life, filled with a strange power. Maybe this Hiram *would* have the guts to run away!

"Fust, folks, Cecil here'll give us a song!" The old fiddler came forward; the fiddle bow quivered and leapt.

> "Oh I danced all night an' my heel kep' a-rockin',
>   My heel kep' a-rockin',
>   My heel kep' a-rockin',
> An' I danced with a gal with a hole in her stockin',
>   The purtiest gal in the room!"

More applause—then shouts of "Let's go!"

"All right, folks, which'll it be—'Duck fer the Oyster,' or 'Down th' Center an' Back'?"

" 'Duck fer the Oyster,' " came back thunderously.

"Partners, find yer places," Hiram boomed. "*One* more couple, *one* more couple!" he called and urged, as the sets filled up.

Johnny looked wistfully around the barn. Sue Ellen was already gobbled up, but there was Eleanor Bartram being pulled forward against her will by Jim Shout. Johnny hated him on sight—a fat bully whom he always detested.

"Eleanor . . . dance with me?"

Someway, he hardly knew how, she had shaken off

Jim and was coming trustingly, her hand in his. At the last minute they slid into place in a set made up by oldsters, but oldsters who could dance, by jiminy! Johnny knew they were thinking, These children'll mess up the set, but they smiled benevolently for all that.

"Circle to the right, circle to the left!"

The big wheel went round and round, as Hiram boomed out the changes. Now the smell of dust and heat—the wild, compelling lilt of "The White Cockade."

> "Fust couple lead to the right,
> Four hands round,
> Duck fer the oyster!"

Forward went the first couple in perfect unison, ducking down under a high arch of upraised hands formed by the second couple, ducking down, then dancing back.

"And now fer the clam!"

Again they moved forward, swiftly and gracefully under the arch. Not a false shuffle. Not a beat of the rhythm missed.

"Right on through to the Promised Land!"

This time under, and on. Now all the couples whirled into the intricate pattern of "allemande left."

Some time it took Johnny to learn this figure, to find one must go "round the corner" before turning and following the chain of hands in reverse. He was confused indeed, bumbling about, feeling lost, and truly messing things up. But Eleanor seized him firmly by the shoulders; someone else gave him a poke. Now he was weaving with the best of them, then marching his girl around in the grand finale of the "promenade." To seize Eleanor by the waist and dance round and round with her, what could be more fun than this, short of heaven?

Johnny never knew how many dances he learned that night, from "Duck fer the Oyster" to "Hawky Fly Out." Every time he could find a place he danced—always with Eleanor, if possible; if not, with anyone he could grab. By refusing to be a member of the head couple, he could watch the figure till his turn came. By that time he had a fair idea of the pattern.

At last the music died away. Hot and weary, the crowd milled about two cider barrels, while the young and tireless drifted out to the moonlit field. Almost in a dream Johnny found himself wandering hand in hand with Eleanor. How sweet she looked, her blue dress misty in the cool light! Cool the little hand, too, that lay relaxed in his. But in his own veins there ran a new fire, which he had never known before—a restlessness, an urgency which had the intensity of pain. What was it? What had come over him? What was the meaning of this strange, new feeling? When the music began again, they returned to the dancing.

All night long the hot, sweet, compelling rhythms, but then at last the dance was ending with two giant Virginia reels. Around the big barn door the crowd shuffled and re-shuffled; couples that had been separated found each other; swains chose their own for the homeward trek.

Jim Bartram offered his arm to Jane; Hiram at once claimed Sue Ellen. Johnny glanced across the crowd to the

place where Eleanor stood waiting. Her blue eyes searched the crowd wistfully. Was she looking for him? He started forward, then stopped, hesitated, and lost his chance. This time Jim Shout bore her off in triumph. Disgusted, crestfallen, he tagged after Hiram and Sue Ellen.

The next day poor Johnny ran the gamut of his family's scorn.

"Too scared to take Eleanor home!" This from Jane.

"What's the matter, Johnny? Did she jilt you, or what?" This was Hiram's offering. Johnny felt his cheeks grow hot. For a few magic moments he had been a man last night; now he was an uncertain, baffled child again, self-doubting . . . and unhappy.

"Think I'd take her home an' come back all by myself in th' dark?" he blurted out. "Not me. Not by the graveyard!"

"Idiot! There was moonlight."

"That made it worse!" said Johnny.

Chapter 6

A BRIGHT MORNING IN MAY, THREE DAYS AFTER THE
square dance. Johnny let his glance stray across intervening
desks to the place where Eleanor sat stooped over her
schoolwork. School, but the four walls vanished. Once
more he seemed to smell the dust of the old barn, hear the
shuffling feet moving to the gay call of the fiddle. How
pretty her yellow hair was, flowing in loose curls about her
shoulders! Could he make her turn around?

As if in answer to a powerful summons, Eleanor lifted
and turned her head. Johnny felt a curious tingling in his
spine as blue eyes met gray in a long, understanding look.
There might have been no one else in the room. She
liked him, he knew, even though he hadn't squired her
home from the dance. Then she smiled and glanced away,
and from far off the teacher's voice broke intrusively upon
his dreams.

"John Burroughs . . . John Burroughs . . . *John
Burroughs!*"

Johnny jumped guiltily. Boys and girls about him were
tittering openly, as he came to belated attention and heard
Mr. Oliver say, "I have called you three times, John Bur-

roughs! Are you deaf . . . or lost? Will you please come forward?"

What now! What had he done? Couldn't a fellow even think his own thoughts? Slowly he climbed to his feet. Thrusting back his shoulders, he stalked down the aisle. Jay Gould and Hi Bouton were already standing in front of the teacher. And Mr. Oliver didn't look displeased.

"More inattentive than usual today, John Burroughs," he said, "but I am happy to inform you boys that your work in arithmetic has been so excellent that I am now promoting you to a new subject. At Squire Ed Burhans' corner store you will find algebras on sale. I have ordered them for each of you. Manage to get yours and bring it to school, by tomorrow if you can. That will do, gentlemen."

Over and over that afternoon on his long hike home from school Johnny found himself wondering how much an algebra book would cost. That was something old Oliver had failed to tell them. As he dashed into the back door of the big white farmhouse, he knew by the noise from the weaving room that his mother was there. Better ask Ma first, he thought, where a new expense was at stake.

All the little room seemed to quiver and shake from the straining of the loom; then, bringing the weaving to a standstill, she smiled up at him. "What is it, Johnny?"

"Got to go to Roxbury, Ma. Any errands?"

"Best take th' mare, dear. Pete's cast a shoe, and Prince is overworked as 'tis."

"Yes, Ma. What'll I get for you?"

"Wal, let me think. I do need a gallon o' 'lasses. Nutmeg and cinnamon is all out too. Your pa needs 'baccy."

"Oh, I'll get *that*—sure!" It would never do to forget so basic an item.

"Ma?"

"Yes, dear?"

"Mr. Oliver says, can I buy an algebra?"

"An algebra!" Amy Kelly looked puzzled and thoughtful. "What'll it be for now?"

"It's a new kind of arithmetic, Ma."

"Isn't the old one still good?"

"I've finished it," John explained firmly. "All learned, over and done with. Now I'm going into a new subject. I'm promoted, because of excellent work, Mr. Oliver says."

"Wal, that's good. Of course you should have your algebra. Better ask Pa, though. Tell him you want some money. I think he's out in the stable, seein' to Pete."

Amy Kelly squared her tired shoulders and shook her head slightly, as if she might shake away besetting burdens; then her feet sought the treadles; back and forth went the flying shuttle. For a moment Johnny watched her, feeling curiously troubled. Feeling, too, that for once she had failed him in a way he couldn't define.

The whole place seemed to reek with the pungent smell of liniment when John found his father in Pete's stall. "Hoss hurt bad, Pa?" he inquired carefully.

"Cast a shoe," Chauncey Burroughs answered. "Didn't notice it soon enough; let him work himself lame."

That was stupid, John thought to himself. But he picked up the rough brown foreleg tenderly, gentling the old work horse as he did so. "Not much swelling as I can see. Maybe just a rest, Pa."

"Mebbe."

It was not the time—no, definitely *not* the time—to ask a favor, but after all, what could he do? Stammering a little, Johnny began slowly. "M-Ma says, will I take the mare and ride to Roxbury for her? That all right, Pa?"

"Fer as I know," his father answered gloomily.

"And I'll get your 'baccy, Pa."

"Yep, I do need some." The tone was slightly mollified.

"C-can I have some change, Pa?"

A frown overshadowed the ruddy, freckled face. "Wal" —one brown, work-hardened hand dug down into the shapeless trousers—"here's a few coppers. That'll do, I reckon."

This wasn't the time to break the news—and yet . . . "Mr. Oliver says, will I b-buy an algebra?"

Hardly had he said the words when he wished them unsaid. For a moment there was a strained and dreadful silence, but Johnny knew it was the calm before the storm. And now the storm broke.

"Of all the numbskulls!" Chauncey bellowed. "That James Oliver! What in tarnation thunder *be* an algebra? Never heerd o' one in all my born days. O' course you can't buy one. Think I got money to throw around on fiddle-faddles?"

"But, *Pa* . . ."

"Be still!" thundered his father in rising fury. "Hiram never had one, nor Curt, nor Wilson. No, nor never asked fer one neither. You may take to larnin', but this be goin' too far. No, I say, no, no, no! Now git out o' my sight!"

Poor Johnny! He had anticipated trouble, but this was too much. He had been proud of his promotion, but there was no use expecting his father and mother to understand. He'd get that algebra, though, by jiminy, if he had to trade everything he owned for it.

What was there to trade, when one came down to it? Not his knife. It was blunted and old. Not his homemade fishing cord, or his battered books, or the fur-trimmed cap, still treasured, though worn and moth-eaten. Up in the attic, carefully hidden away, was a small store of maple-sugar cakes, left from his last batch. They were pure white sugar, which he had boiled to perfection himself. Once more Johnny sought the back door of his home. Swiftly he conquered two flights of stairs. When he rode the mare Hardscrabble way, the last of his sugar rode, carefully wrapped, in a saddlebag beside him.

As he kicked at the mare's flanks and urged her into a slow canter, he thought he heard his father's voice again, booming out far behind him. "Johnny," he distinctly made out. "Come back, Johnny!" Had Pa relented after all? Had Ma met him and talked him into a grudging and belated consent? Most likely. It had happened before. But this time, John told himself, it would be by his own efforts. Perhaps it was about time that he managed things for himself.

The yellow corner store in Roxbury Village was a lavish, fascinating center to Johnny's country eyes. Here fancy stocks sat side by side with cassimere or cologne; solemn Bibles hobnobbed with humble groceries. Quietly he waited at a counter while two strange farmers bought timothy seed, currycombs, and the inevitable tobacco. A tall, slender girl was serving them with an efficiency which

Johnny admired. Now she moved over to the woman's corner, still keeping him waiting. But this sale went briskly, as whalebones and calico crossed the counter. Soon she slid back to face him and surprised him with a pleasant "Well, John Burroughs, something I can do for you?"

"You know my n-n-name?"

"Seen you at church, or else"—she corrected the statement, while a dimple appeared at the corner of her lips and a mischievous flash in her eyes—"at the Old School Baptist picnic." Johnny began to think that he'd better improve his churchgoing. "And seen you at the square dance in the Hollow, too!" she added.

"W-what's your name?"

"Mary Taft," she answered pleasantly.

"Squire Burhans not here?"

"Not just now."

Johnny began to think that his absence was providential. Surely this pleasant girl could be more easily argued into the virtues of a trade. First he made the family purchases. Then slowly and a bit hesitantly he unwrapped his pile of white delectable cakes to spread them out before her on the counter. Haltingly he told his story—how he had sold the rest of his sugar early; what he thought it was worth in fair and honest value; how he had kept some back, hoping to use it for a special purpose. And now, needing the algebra, and finding it inconvenient for his family . . .

Perhaps Mary Taft did not have the authority to make the trade; perhaps she did not know the value of an algebra. But she did understand the importance of young ambition and pride. As she looked up into the sensitive face with its eager eyes (Were they blue or gray? How deep and glowing they were!) she felt that nothing in the world could make her refuse this request.

"Here's the algebra, Johnny," she said. "If 'tisn't right with Squire, he'll tell you later. I'm sure we can sell your cakes. Come see us again soon, won't you?"

"You bet I will," said John, lingering on for no apparent reason, unless it was to see that dimple once more, or the gay, sidelong glance which went with it. He took a good look at her before he turned away. How long and black her lashes were! How pale and colorless little Eleanor seemed beside her dark beauty!

More than maple cakes and an algebra went in exchange that day.

John Burroughs at fifteen was hungry for life both in and out of books. *Murphy the Indian Killer* held him spellbound, but he liked even better to follow a trout stream or hunt on the hills. He was like a spirited young colt— eager, restless, full of a vast curiosity, long-legged and sound of wind.

Never'd make a farmer—that one. No, siree! his father thought as he watched him work. Head in th' clouds! But he kept him out of school every summer now just the same, proving his use to the farm. Couldn't he saw wood, hoe out his row in the garden, keep the plow to a straight furrow, and swing a scythe with the best of them? But then, when you wanted him, he was like quicksilver. Suddenly he wa'n't there. Up in the woods most likely, peerin' at a bird's nest.

Hiram, ten years older, still on the farm, was wonderful with his hands. He could make anything from ox yokes to sleds. Curtis was a swift, expert milker. Each boy had his special gifts. But Johnny—what'd he ever 'mount to?

It was late Saturday afternoon of a clear, cold fall day. Johnny, freed from many chores, had begun school again for the winter term, but this was Saturday. One good moment of freedom! Gun in hand, he could climb through the sugarbush and on to the long, welcoming slopes of Old Clump. The woods were alive with color—scarlet and gold and deep somber maroon. His feet rustled the dry leaves and he tried to quiet them. Surely everything would hear him coming.

By this time he was an expert shot. Long ago, as a little boy, he had been taught to keep the chipmunks away from his father's corn, the woodchucks from the garden. Hadn't his brothers rolled pumpkins downhill toward him so he could practice shooting?

Hark! What was that distant high yelp, followed by a low, mournful baying? A fox—and a hound after him. Excited and thrilled, Johnny rammed in the shot. Coming this way, closer now, that intermittent cry that was the very spirit of wildness. Shivering in the keen fall wind off the mountain, he stood and waited. Was the breeze carrying his scent? Would the fox be warned and double back on his tracks?

The call came again, fainter and far more distant, the bark that was like a dog's but never continuous as a dog's was. The hound had fallen silent. Perhaps he'd lost the scent, for a fox was a clever customer, wise enough to run a line of high stone wall or hide in a hollow tree trunk. He knew how to baffle his four-legged hunter.

Shivering in the bitter wind, Johnny fished for the warm mittens in his pocket and drew them on. Then he waited and waited, numb with discouragement and cold. What was the use? As he turned to go, the leaves rustled; there came the sharp crack of a broken twig. Across the small clearing in front of him a huge red fox loped along at ease. Dark legs beneath a superb, proud body, a magnificent, white-tipped brush floating out behind as if carried by its own lightness.

Fascinated, Johnny stood and watched, held spellbound by the animal's matchless beauty, its swift, easy motion. In an instant, all unconscious of the watcher, the fox had cleared the opening, bounded with one graceful leap into the forest, and was gone.

Then and not till then Johnny came to himself. Shocked and disgusted, he remembered the gun in his hands. He had simply forgotten to shoot. Could he ever face the ridicule that would meet him at home?

When he did get home and the boys teased him, he had only one answer. "Aw—shucks! Couldn't get my mitten off in time!"

But years afterward, as he recalled the incident, he was apt to say that he had carried away the best part of the fox after all, a picture of living beauty and freedom that he could not bear to kill.

John stood watching Hiram as he led old Brock out of the stable by one of his long, gleaming, wide-spreading

horns. Deftly he lifted the heavy yoke, took out the key that held in the bow, eased one end of the yoke on Brock's shoulder and the bow round his neck. Holding the other end of the great yoke, he called to Johnny, "Help me out, will you, feller? Bring out Bright, quick now!" In an instant Johnny had helped lift the birch yoke end on to Bright's patient back. Now the bow was fastened, the key put in to hold it, and the two beasts moved off ponderously, pulling the stoneboat behind them.

"Coming along to help?" Hi shouted back over his shoulder as he raised the gad.

"Nope," said Johnny, "Pa didn't say to." And I'm *not* going unless he does, he might have added, but kept that to himself.

Strange as it seemed, and much as he loved his kindly older brother, he found himself pitying Hi. Long ago Hi had stopped talking about gold and forty-niners and how any minute he would run away to join them. For a long time the carpetbag still lay ready under the bed, but last week it had gone. Johnny knew then that the small flickering candle of Hi's dream had burned itself out. Poor Hi, he thought. He couldn't even speak to him about it! If he would only show resentment or anger, or a little spunk! 'Twasn't right always to be so cheerful!

As for himself, he was ready to fight with everyone today, this first day of summer when Pa had told him, "From now on you'll stay home from school." He liked school. It was play to him and an escape from drudgery he hated. Books held the key which might unlock the door to another world. He liked learning, not hauling stones for a wall. But what could he do about it? When could he be his own master?

He turned away from the stable and moved swiftly and quietly up the sloping hill, along the edges of the great pasture till he came to the spot which most of all he loved, the big rock at the eastern end of the farm, near what was called the Rundle place.

As a child he had loafed and rested here, and now as a youngster it was his special place in which to brood and dream. Not the childish dreams of other years. He no longer expected to be rich, to buy all the land below him. Nor would he bring jewels and fine dresses to his mother. What use would she have of them if he did? But it was easy to dream of the land beyond the mountains. How little he knew of it! A few butter trips to Catskill, one three-day hike to Lexington to see his married sister, Olly—these were his few brief contacts with a world he longed for.

It was easy to dream of other schools and other friends; of girls who were prettier even than Eleanor Bartram or Mary Taft. Easy to long for Harpersfield, where Dick Van Dyke had gone, or Franklin Institute, or Cooperstown. When could he escape? Would it be *when* . . . or never?

Climbing the rock, he stretched himself upon its hard, cool surface. Something of its own strength seemed to enter into him, something of its peace.

Too bad he had promised his teacher to be in school today. He was just at the end of his algebra and . . . a new teacher, Josiah Gilbert, one he liked—tall, handsome, and athletic, and not afraid to be friendly. Why, he had even shown the fellows some new wrestling holds after school one day. He wasn't much older than they were anyway. Just out of Franklin Literary Institute himself.

Gee whittakers! Suddenly Johnny snapped out of his mournful, loafing mood and slid down the rock with eagerness. He'd almost forgotten. Old Josh had asked him to tell his mother he was coming to stay with them this week, since it was the Burroughs' turn to board him. He'd *better* tell her, or the schoolmaster would starve! Gathering speed, like a long-legged colt, he sprinted downhill toward the farmhouse.

Just as the whole family had settled noisily down around the supper table that night, there came a brisk knock at the door. Cuff barked, John dropped his knife with a clatter and tried to slide from his place on the bench, but Abigail was ahead of him. In the doorway stood the schoolmaster, satchel in hand.

"Come in, sir, and welcome!" Amy Kelly called, rising from her chair and greeting him with outstretched hands. "Our fare is simple, but there's plenty of it. Fresh apple pie, and milk still warm, or shall I make you tea or coffee, sir?"

That night, as they sat around the fire in the big fireplace, the young schoolmaster studied their faces with inquiring eyes. How quiet they all were! *Taciturn*, he thought to himself. Was the Burroughs family always like this, or did his presence make them shy? Chauncey, the father, smoking his pipe with steady, even puffs. Amy Kelly, head bent over a mending basket. Even young Abigail diligently sewing calico squares for a new comfortable. Only Johnny, encamped on the floor beside him, seemed to be unoccupied; but he, too, was quiet.

"Mr. Burroughs"—the young man turned toward the freckled-faced, swarthy farmer—"this son of yours is a mighty promising scholar."

Slowly Chauncey Burroughs withdrew his pipe, said, "Yep—mebbe," and put it back again.

But Amy Kelly dropped her mending back into the basket and looked up eagerly. "Johnny's always took to larnin', Mr. Gilbert. Seems to be the main thing he does take to. But schooling's got to come to an end some time."

"Must it, ma'am?" asked the tall guest warmly. "Shouldn't come to an end for a boy like this. My own Institute where I have been trained would admit him gladly. Perhaps you will let me recommend . . ."

Johnny's cheeks began to burn. Pa wouldn't stand for this, he knew, not for long. And indeed at that instant the testy, quick-tempered farmer rose to his feet. One moment he hesitated, turning the ashes out of his pipe and tapping it, bowl upside down on the mantelpiece. Then he turned to the schoolmaster, his face crimson. In a rough voice he cried, "Mr. Gilbert, you mean it kindly and I thank you for that. When I want advice as to my son's eddication, I'll come to you—and not before. There's one man and one only who makes the rules at this place, and that's meself. Amy, give this young man his tallow dip and show him to his room. 'Tis high time fer bed. Good night, sir!"

Startled by the rudeness, but not hurt on his own account, the teacher turned to look at Johnny, who still sat cross-legged on the floor beside him. For a brief moment their glances crossed. In his own eyes stood a troubled pity, but on Johnny's face he saw such blazing anger and defiance that he moved back, troubled. Can't blame him, he thought. The boy must show fight to gain his independence. He has the spirit and the ambition. Will he have the courage, too?

Perhaps, even though rejected at the time, the schoolmaster's words had had their effect. Perhaps Amy Kelly had spoken a more convincing word at some quiet moment. Perhaps Johnny's own work this summer was proving an argument in his favor. At any rate, not many days later, as he hauled stones for Hiram at the wall building, suddenly Pa dropped a hand on his shoulder.

"Work like a nailer, Johnny," he said. "Hew to the line this summer . . . and then . . . I'll send you away to school in the fall."

Chapter 7

ALL THE SUMMER OF HIS SIXTEENTH YEAR JOHNNY DID
indeed "work like a nailer." First he helped with the wall
building and the sheep shearing. Every morning and evening he did his share of the milking. He drove the cows to
pasture and at night he collected them again. And always
there were chores to be done about the stable and pasture—
barn cleaning, manure spreading, stump burning. Now,
during the long weeks of haying at the hottest time of the
year, Johnny took his place with the men, swinging his
scythe through meadow after meadow.

John felt, himself, that he learned a great deal that summer—learned how to stick to a job, keep his mouth shut,
and not complain. Work was easy when it was done for the
sake of winning his right to Harpersfield. There was fun,
too, plenty of it, along the way; now and then a barn raisin'
or an apple cut or, gayest of all, a square dance. Or the evening for which he longed most of all when he could call on
his girl in the village. Blonde Eleanor Bartram's star had
dropped below the horizon, but Mary Taft's radiance rode
high.

One Sunday night, not long after his father's promise, Johnny started out to walk to Roxbury for his usual call at the little red house. Not every Sunday—that wouldn't do. That meant going steady, and Pa didn't approve of it. But this was the right evening and even Ma didn't have a word to say.

Soon he settled back on the opposite side of the hearth from Mary, looking across to the place where she sat so demurely, wishing he could shorten the distance. How pretty she was! The full red lips with the dimple coming and going at the corner of them as she talked or smiled. How easily she smiled! He wished as he watched her that he could kiss that dimple, then pulled himself back from the thought wistfully. Perhaps when he had come back from Harpersfield?

Sometimes they chatted aimlessly, and sometimes long silences stood between them. It was easy and comfortable to keep silent with Mary. She didn't mind. Their eyes found each other's, and there was understanding in the long glance.

At twelve o'clock she sighed a little and went to the kitchen, while he stooped to mend the neglected fire. Now the pleasant clatter of pans and glasses, and Mary's triumphant return with cider and cake. A wonderful cake she had made herself, thick with rich maple-sugar frosting. The whole room seemed filled with its hot, spicy fragrance. Like hungry wolves, like greedy children, they discussed it. If he touched her hand as she passed the food to him, a curious thrill came to him. Once he clung to the hand and pulled her toward him, but she twisted away laughing.

Suddenly it was two o'clock, and that, Johnny knew, meant good night.

She came to the door with him and stood looking out at the moonlight. Misty and cool, it touched the village street softly and gave to each roof a sharp, black line.

"Pretty night!" Mary said.

"Not the only pretty thing," John answered, longing to be more daring. For a moment she looked up at him. Gently she laid one hand upon his arm; her red lips parted a little and the hand on his arm tightened. Then she said, "Good night, Johnny," and the door closed swiftly.

With a wistful sense of loss, John stumbled down the steps to the road. What did he want? He couldn't make love yet—"too young," they told him. It was dreadful to be always too young.

The walk back that night, Hardscrabble way, seemed endless. Yes, here was the sharp turn up from the village. Here the stone schoolhouse where he had had his first lessons. How tiny it looked! It was a lovely night, filled with a kind of mystic radiance. The hills were walls of black, the air heady with sweetness, as he passed the farmhouses where lilacs bloomed. Now the little graveyard with its crooked stones. He *must* go by it before he could reach the farm.

As he walked swiftly on, he heard, or thought he heard, a soft noise behind him, the sound of a cautious footstep. He quickened his pace, and the soft padding sound gained speed too. Now a rapid trot, turning into a desperate, panic-stricken running. All the horrible tales of his grandfather about the "haunts" in this same graveyard came

back to plague and torment him. What dreadful thing
was following him? Would it overtake and destroy him?

In an instant John had become a tortured, terrified child,
as he tore breathlessly along the country road. But soon a
hard inner core of sense came back to sustain him. "Silly!"
something inside him said. "You're being a baby again.
Those tales of Granther's were pure invention and you
know it. There's nothing behind you now that wouldn't
be here in daylight. *Turn around and see.*"

Summoning all his courage and self-respect, Johnny
stopped and swung about. Fearing to look, but forcing
himself to the task, he studied the winding roadway behind
him. A misty line of silver clear and empty in the moonlight. Beyond that—nothing. Sheepish and ashamed,
Johnny hurried on. Yet he knew, too, that he had won a
victory that night, a final victory over the inheritance of
fear which Granther had bequeathed to him.

As the summer wore on, it seemed to Johnny that more
and more disagreeable tasks were dropped in his lap, or
handed to him at the end of a hoe. Then came the day when
Pa asked him to plow the side-hill lot above the sap bush,
cross-plowing to prepare the ground for winter rye.

"But, Pa, that's practically virgin field—full o' rocks an'
stumps."

Chauncey Burroughs scratched his thick, carroty hair
thoughtfully. "A bit o' dynamite'll do th' trick. Get Hi
to help. Little rocks can be drugged out. Best plow round
the biggest."

Johnny started to answer, then clamped his lips together

tight. Wasn't he a grown man going to Harpersfield? Like Dick Van Dyke from last year's class, he'd soon be off and away.

Through the hot September days he followed Prince and Pete across the rough field, stumbling into great holes, yawning wounds from which the stones had been torn. The handles of the plow jerked and jumped, blistering even his work-hardened hands. But someway, he didn't mind too greatly.

As he worked, he listened to the music of the meadow larks, soaring above him, or noted the rhythm of the shadows weaving across Old Clump. Now the end of his plow touched a nest at the edge of the field and a tiny white-footed deer mouse scampered away, the young clinging to her teats. So fast she jumped that some of the babies fell, but she came back anxiously to pick them up one by one, carrying them by the nape of the neck as a cat carries kittens. Amused and moved by the creature's pygmy courage, Johnny stayed his plow and stopped to watch. He must tell Mary about it, he thought. Motherhood in miniature!

So he plowed with hope, making deep, straight furrows across the field. So he plowed on, and dreams were his companions.

The red of fall was already in the sugar maples when Johnny plucked up his courage to question Chauncey Burroughs. "Pa, most time for Harpersfield, isn't it? When can I go?"

The usually blustering farmer seemed strangely silent. One brown hand sought the pocket of his jeans to pull out

a wad of tobacco which he turned in his fingers . . . slowly . . . slowly . . . dark eyes fixed thoughtfully on the twisting fingers.

"Wal . . ." There was a long silence, and Johnny waited with a growing anxiety. "Truth is, boy . . . hate to say it. You done right smart work this summer, but . . . I'd send you now if I could. Fact is, John, I just ain't got th' money."

"But, Pa, you *promised!*"

"Yep . . . back last spring . . . didn't know price of butter wouldn't hold. Didn't know Olly Ann 'ud write fer money. Go to West Settlement this winter, Johnny. It's a good school," he pleaded wistfully.

Choking back the sobs, Johnny tore across the fields—off—away—anywhere—anyhow—to hide his misery and fight with his despair. Now he lay stretched face down on his great rock, the blue sky shut away, hands clutching at the cold solidity of the stone.

Pa had tricked him. Pa had given his word and tricked him. Let him hope for Harpersfield all the long summer through. Wave on wave of bitterness rolled over him. Men don't cry, he told himself, even as he tasted the salt upon his lips. In the midst of his misery something soft touched his hand, a low whining stole up to him. Now a cold, wet muzzle against his ear. Old Cuff. Too lame to come up the hill easily, but knowing someway that Johnny needed him.

He put his arm around the shaggy neck, finding a sudden resource in the old dog's devotion, smoothing the rough coat with the inevitable burrs caught in it, smoothing his own way back to self-control.

Acceptance? Not yet, perhaps, but self-control, at least.

When Johnny came into the house in Roxbury on Sunday night, Mary knew at once that something was wrong. "John," she cried, putting out both hands to him, "you're all upset over something!"

He told her then, and indeed she knew, how he had been hoping to go to Harpersfield, and now of his bitter disappointment.

"But, Johnny," she cried, after she had listened to the story all the way through without comment or interruption, " 'tisn't like you to give up. Surely there's a way. I mean—maybe not now, but . . . don't you remember how you used your own maple sugar to buy the algebra? Isn't there something you can do yourself? There's sure to be a way, Johnny."

"Maybe," said John. "But 'twould take a heap of maple sugar, Mary."

That winter when John was sixteen, he went back again to the West Settlement school, went obediently, since his mother and father asked it. But he was restless and bored. Same old subjects! The boys were too young and the girls uninteresting. Same old algebra! Yet he was not deceived. Other books might be thrilling and wonderful. Other books, the names of which he did not even know, might be keys to turn in his hand, might be doors to the future.

At night, though he usually slept the sleep of the young and weary, sometimes he squirmed restlessly in the feather bed and Eden, protesting, shoved an elbow in his side. Tonight was such a night. Through wide-open eyes he stared into the darkness.

What would he ever be? What would he come to? A farmer, like his father? He'd be a middlin' poor farmer! A stay-at-home, like Hiram? Married—and too poor, like Olly? Again he thought, as he often had before, of Mary Taft's words: "Surely there's something you can do for yourself, John!" But there wasn't—not a thing. This was a blind wall. This was a suffocating fog.

Then a thought came to him. Beyond the mountains, down in the little town of Olive, near the Hudson River country, was a man named Dr. Hull, whom the family knew and loved. Amy Kelly often talked of his kindness, his love of children, his long hard hours of doctoring, his sacrificial life. *He* would help a fellow—yes—sure!

Acting on impulse, Johnny plunged through the darkness, down the creaking stairs to the kitchen. The bellows complained, but blew up the sparks. Taking paper from his black oilskin bag, ink and a quill from the mantelpiece, he squatted down before the fire, and the shadows kept him company.

To Dr. Hull of the town of Olive;

Esteemed Sir: (He wrote, in his best sloping, angular handwriting.)

I now take pen in hand to ask . . . (and he concluded, as all good letter writers should) I remain, Sir, your humble and obedient servant, John Burroughs. (But then he added as postscript one simple line full of boyish urgency.) I beg you, Sir, to reply by Return Post.

While Johnny squatted on the floor writing, far away
across the intervening miles another young man, in his
early thirties, sat facing pen and paper. Sat in a small, airless bedroom in Brooklyn, writing at a plain deal table,
burdened only with a litter of notebooks and papers. He
was a tall man with a big powerful body and the work-
hardened hands of an artisan. Brooding eyes of a dreamer
and thinker seemed out of place above the hands. On the
wall before him hung a plain card, on which were neatly
printed the words: "Now make the Works."

The slogan seemed to please him, for now and then he
smiled up at it. Sometimes he seemed to take its advice and
write feverishly; sometimes he dropped his pen and stared
listlessly into space. He had been an editor, and the art of
writing was not new to him. But that was journalism; that
was different; that was easy, day-by-day stuff, talk of the
market place. He was out of a job now, disillusioned with
newspapers, weary of politics, weary even of the bright,
Bohemian young men loafing along Broadway. They had
been his pals—yes—sure. But not now.

He would write the poetry of which he had always
dreamed—songs of a new land, its vigor and greatness, its
heritage . . . and destiny. He would write of the common
man, the humble man, the worker, whose toil and hopes
built the future; of man in general, en masse . . . yes, and
of himself as the symbol of man. Of *himself* . . . of all
the nameless, mystic, incoherent yearnings which welled
up from some strange depth within him. He would write
of the body and of the soul, for were not matter and spirit
one?

"I am the poet of the Body and I am the poet of the
Soul, . . .

.   .   .

I am the poet of the woman the same as the man,
And I say it is as great to be a woman as to be a man,
And I say there is nothing greater than the mother of
men."

Across the intervening miles, Walt Whitman sat writing.

Far away in Illinois another young man sat that night
with long legs stretched to the dwindling fire of a country
inn. He had been riding hard all day; he would face a dull
and petty case tomorrow. What, after all, did it matter?
Pettifogging, that was all!

Well, he had had his moment of greatness—been in
Washington, no less! But now that was over. The people
had spoken; they had not returned him. Where and why
had he failed? Here he was, back again, set in the stirrups
of a nameless country lawyer. A look of pain seemed to
etch deeper lines beside the firm, kindly mouth, and the
eyes in the homely face were filled with a melancholy,
brooding look.

A young man banged open the door suddenly and rushed
toward him with all the vigor of a spring freshet. "Come
to bed, Abe, old fellow!" he cried, then failed to continue,
for the man in the chair, smiling impishly, stretched out
one long leg and tripped him neatly.

"Abe, how long should a man's legs be?" he blurted out,
recovering himself quickly.

"Wal . . . long enough to reach the ground, I reckon," answered the man called Abe. "Git on, Bill. I got to do a heap of thinkin' tonight."

Left alone at last, he thrust a hand into the half-open carpetbag beside him. Out came Euclid and soon the man's eager mind sought the anodyne of hard and knotty problems. Euclid, so difficult, so fascinating—he loved it!

But yawning at last, he dropped the little book and fished for another. *The Merchant of Venice* now, though he knew it already from cover to cover. But savoring the words, he read softly aloud to himself:

> "The quality of mercy is not strain'd,
>   It droppeth as the gentle rain from heaven . . ."

Abe Lincoln, Walt Whitman—and John Burroughs. The boy and the two men were to meet in the years ahead at a time and place forever known to history. Each was to influence, to give meaningful help to one of the others. Each, in his own peculiar way, would contribute to the freedom of the human spirit.

Long before daylight on a cold March morning, Johnny woke up and stared into the darkness. What was special about this morning? Why did he feel excited and yet, someway, frightened? Then he remembered. This was the day, *this was the day*, when he had promised himself to take the long, hard hike over Batavia Mountain. No one was going with him. He must go alone.

For a moment he ducked back under the covers and

waited, feeling warm and safe and half-determined to stay there. The next moment he was chiding himself and plunging into his clothes. Down the stairs now, seeking the half-light and warmth of the kitchen. In the dim glow of the candle Ma stood, a tall and shadowy figure, brisking up the fire. How welcome the smell of coffee boiling, fat pork sizzling, and flapjacks putting their delicious brown jackets on! A swift sense of home and comfort, of the goodness of all familiar things, almost broke down his brave resolve.

Then he blurted out, "Too early for you, Ma!"

"No, it's all right, Johnny!" She turned then and seized his arm, giving it an unusual tight squeeze. "Wish I could go with you. But you'll like Dr. Hull."

"Think he'll help me find a school to teach, Ma?"

"He'll do his best, Johnny. He wrote you to come, didn't he?"

"Yep, and I'm going," Johnny answered, with a decisiveness he didn't feel.

"Wal, set an' eat. Got to have something to walk on."

He had already finished when, one by one, the rest of the family straggled in, standing in a little group around him, as he packed his few possessions in the black oilcloth carpetbag with the rounded metal top. It wouldn't hold much. Just as well, since 'twould be heavy to lug. Extra socks, of course, and another shirt (he was already wearing two for warmth) and at the last minute he added his battered algebra. Hard to tell why, except that in some strange way he was proud of it and it just might impress some school trustee.

They all watched him, strangely silent and subdued. No

scoffing or fool advice, even from Curt or Wilson, and, strangest of all, not a word from Pa. Then suddenly young Adelaide threw her arms around him. "Oh, Johnny," she cried, "you won't b-be here for your b-birthday. D-don't go, Johnny!"

It was at this point that Pa came to life. "Don't blubber, Adelaide!" he said severely. "Wal, good-by, son," he went on less gruffly. "Mind you watch the blazes on the mountain and don't take no blind turns. I'm proud of you, son!" he added, with a new respect in his voice.

But not proud enough to give me a lift on my way, Johnny thought to himself. But, for all that, he looked his father straight in the eyes and smiled. "Good-by, Pa. Hope I don't have to come back. I'll do my best to find a school to teach. Good-by, Ma!"

"You come back if you need to, Johnny," she cried. "Come back often, dear," she added, with such love and warmth in the tone and such longing in her lined and tired face that again John was hard put to it to stay firm and manly.

Once more his eyes sought the circle of family faces. Something missing. Where was Hiram, whom most of all he loved—half father, half brother—and always kind. He *must* say good-by to him. Was he staying away because he was angry, or envious? Not Hi! That was incredible.

At this moment the back door opened and Hi came sauntering in out of the shadows. "Wal, Johnny, most missed you, didn't I? Want to wish you luck—and here's a lucky piece to say it." He dug deep in his breeches' pocket and fished up a coin, holding it out to Johnny with stained brown fingers. For an instant it caught the candlelight and flashed—a silver dollar, a whole, bright silver dollar.

"Oh, no!" Johnny cried. "It's too m-much. You'll n-need it, Hi!" As always the fatal stammer when he was greatly moved.

"Thought so onct—but I don't need it none now. Take it, feller—an' good luck!" His big brown hand gave Johnny's shoulder a kindly push.

Out the door now, and starting on his way. At the end it was Cuff who made the going hardest, for he came lumbering after him, whining and limping down the stone steps. Eden had to catch and hold him before the old dog would give up.

Swinging his carpetbag, Johnny started up the road, dim and ghostly in the half-light of dawn. The wind still carried the bitter sting of winter, and along the edges of the woods the snowdrifts gleamed white. He cast a glance back over his shoulder, looking for the friendly rounded dome of Old Clump, but the mountain still slept under its blanket of mist and gave him no message of farewell.

On up the road, past the turn into the Deacon path. He remembered how he had escaped as a little fellow and just at this point had desperately run home again. No turning back now! Not now, when he was almost seventeen! He would climb over the saddle of Batavia Mountain and on down into Red Kill. Eight miles would take him to Uncle Martin's, where he could spend the night. Next day he would go to Griffin's Corners and catch the stage for Olive. Clutching his carpetbag, trying to twist his lips into a whistle, he walked firmly on.

Part Two

1854-1865

Quicksand years that whirl me I know not whither,
Your schemes, politics, fail, lines give way, substances mock and
    elude me,
Only the theme I sing, the great and strong-possess'd soul, eludes
    not,
One's-self must never give way—that is the final substance—that
    out of all is sure,
Out of politics, triumphs, battles, life, what at last finally remains?
When shows break up what but One's-Self is sure?

WALT WHITMAN

Chapter 8

So this was his prize! Early on a cold morning in April, Johnny stood looking up at a small red schoolhouse set on a hill, to which he had bound himself for six long months. His prize, his badge of freedom—or his treadmill? Whatever it proved to be, he looked at it now partly in fear and partly in mounting elation. At least it was his, and he could teach as he wished.

It had been hard enough to win. For days he had driven around with the good doctor only to find most of the posts taken, or to meet with a curt "Much too inexperienced." Or what was worst of all, to hear "You're far too young!" Deep in discouragement, he had feared he must crawl back to the farm to eat his humble pie.

But one morning Dr. Hull called to him. "Climb into the buggy! I'm driving to Tongore. There's no teacher there, Johnny, far as I can learn. And for heaven's sake, *smile* at the trustee, boy! You look like a funeral in wintertime!"

Johnny had smiled; the doctor had added a pleasant word or two.

"Ten dollars for the first month and, if he suits, eleven for the other five."

The deal was closed and John Burroughs was the teacher at Tongore.

Now he climbed the path that led to the top of the hill, noting, as he did so, a rushing brook foaming in the deep ravine below him. At the door he looked back a moment to see the pale blue of Olive Mountain and the distant Catskills clear against a spring sky. If he was homesick, uncertain, and anxious, at least the mountains were there, all the good companions of Old Clump.

The central room of the school was cold, dirty, and ugly. The tiny window was filthy, the desk tops crisscrossed with knife marks. And some of the desks rocked as he put his hand on them, holding to the floor with only a single screw. In the corner a pile of switches leaned suggestively.

But a good stack of split logs stood beside the rusty stove. As he built up the fire and heard its cheerful crackle, suddenly he felt at home. How like his own West Settlement school this was, from the deep-cut noon mark on the window sill to the battered old chair on the platform meant for Teacher! *Meant for Teacher!* But how could he ever answer to that name?

He stood in the doorway ringing the bell with long, even strokes, and now he saw small figures running in answer. A little fat girl with blond braids was the first to puff up the hill. She blinked her eyes in surprise as she looked at him.

Here came groups of children. Here an older girl, bringing a little fellow. He smiled when he saw them, remembering his own Hardscrabble School and a small boy with broken slate and "ep-lets." Here, at the very end, three boys who were much too big. Older than himself perhaps, he thought, as he watched their approach.

The first to come, obviously the ringleader, was a thick-set youngster with a knowing sneer on his lips. Pale-blue eyes, above an undershot jaw and thick bull neck. Was it muscle or fat that made him so impressive, John wondered, conscious of a sense of dismay. The typical small-school bully, he decided, and knew that some day, sooner or later, he would come to terms with him.

A tall boy with thin, cadaverous face came next, paying the first one devoted and fawning attention, and a third lad brought up the rear, overgrown and awkward, in a jacket far too short and tight.

"Gee whittakers," the last one cried. "Where in thunder's old Allen?"

"Stupid," the bully answered, kicking him on the shin and making him stumble. "We chased him out, didn' you know?"

When prayers were over, Johnny stood and faced them. "School come to order," he called firmly, as the last amen died away. What should he do now? What was the schedule they were used to? And why did his knees feel weak and the miserable stammer come back to his words?

Somehow the morning wore on. Spelling, arithmetic, reading. The little fellows drilled in the alphabet. Twenty minutes for practice in penmanship—all the usual pattern of the schooling he knew. The children weren't good; they were noisy and restless. But neither were they out of hand. Johnny began to relax and feel more at ease. Why are you afraid of them? he asked himself. That little ten-year-old, with the cornflower blue eyes, might be Adelaide. Those big boys might be Curt and Wilson. What's so terrible about them?

At recess time they all rushed out with the riotous joy of release. Voices which drifted back to Johnny, as he sat eating his apple and rye bread by the stove, sounded happy and well occupied. But when nooning was over, and the stream trickled back again, he felt at once a new atmosphere in the room.

What had happened? Was there some planned strategy afoot? Thirty pairs of eyes gazed back at him in a silence which seemed someway hostile and threatening. Taking up a theme book, he started to give out subjects for a composition. But as he began it, a low hum-m-m-m commenced in a distant corner. Gentle at first, like the drone of buzzing insects, it grew gradually in volume till a steady, insistent roaring seemed to rise and fall in the little room.

"Children, children!" he cried. Handicapped, because as yet he had not learned their names, he called them to order with a firmness he didn't feel. Not a muscle in their faces seemed to quiver; not a single pair of lips moved. But still the steady roaring rose and beat against the schoolroom like surf pounding against a beach.

Disgusted and uncertain, Johnny seated himself, opened his book, and waited. For a while he made a miserable pretense of reading. What else was there to do but ignore the mass attack? He couldn't stop it—or even place the blame for it. They were all alike guilty, and all alike guiltless. Very well, he would wait and see. But well he knew that if a trustee should happen to drop in on the new teacher, this would prove his final day as well as his first one.

Perhaps the children grew tired of their ruse, for now the mood grew wilder. A book banged to the floor here, another there. Small objects began to fly through the air—bits of chalk, even a broken slate pencil. A very little girl, sitting on the small children's bench in front, put her hand to her face and began a dismal wailing. Stooping to comfort her, Johnny saw a big oblong flash through the air, felt a hard blow on the side of his head as the closed pocketknife hit him. Involuntary tears came to his eyes, quick anger to his heart, that Irish anger that was sharp, swift, and hot.

This time he caught a gesture, saw a hand rise to throw, and knew the culprit. Striding down the aisle, he laid ungentle hands on the bully's collar. "Stand up and apologize," he cried. "You have done an unmanly thing to hit a person caught off guard!"

The boy snickered, made a rude noise, and slouched back in his seat, misreading the slenderness and inexperience of the teacher. Beside him the big boys guffawed, the class rocked with laughter.

"Try to make me!" he said.

But the muscles in Johnny's slender arms, trained by the use of plow handle, hoe, and scythe, were strong as steel. Not for nothing had he downed Jay Gould at wrestling. With a terrific wrench he seized the boy and pulled. The youngster clung to his desk, and now his lips went white. But the desk was old, rickety, and insecurely fastened. It, too, gave under the attack. Boy and desk, Johnny dragged them along the floor.

Holding him firmly, the teacher selected a long switch from the waiting pile and plied it, not too hard or too unkindly, across the lad's bent back. But the young bully had the endurance of cowardice and loud roars of protest filled the little schoolroom.

Sick at heart, with anger ebbing fast, Johnny stopped the punishment and sent the boy limping to a seat. With regret, almost with shame, he looked down now at the switch still firmly clasped in his hand. How little this disgraceful scene had been his plan! How different this was from what he had come to do!

With a quick, impulsive gesture he broke the switch in two, dropping the pieces on the floor before him. Absolutely silent now, the children sat and watched him, big-eyed, wondering, as at some show the outcome of which they could not even guess.

"Boys and girls," said Johnny, and now the words came clearly, "I did not come to beat you into learning, but to teach you what you need and wish to know. I have broken this switch and I will break the others. I give you my promise now that they will never again be used. If you will help me, together we can run this school—together—as friends. The day has been long and hard, and the time left is brief. School is now dismissed. You have your assignments. Come back promptly in the morning."

John Burroughs had won his first bout with the children, but well he knew that there would be others just ahead. He was indeed uncertain and inexperienced, as several trustees had quickly guessed. But what the trustees had not seen were qualities which made John a teacher; first the knowledge of different ages which comes from the give and take of a big family, second a real liking for children, and third a definite desire to help them grow.

When the day went badly, as it often did, he trudged off to his boardinghouse at night in deep discouragement. When it went well, there came a glow of satisfaction which he had rarely felt before. Not always did he know what to do. When two of the big boys were caught in a desperate, bloody fight, when one of the little children was taken suddenly ill—these small crises he met as best he could, with what tact and firmness he possessed at the time.

Always he tried to bring interest and freshness to his teaching, not to drone on, or to let the children drag on in the same old patterns. He early persuaded them to bring in bits of news that interested them, or some quotation they liked from the *Farmer's Almanac*, or some fact they had learned about another country. These he wove into a strange hodgepodge session called "class in current events."

When nooning came, he often forgot his lunch and went out to the others on the playground. It was fun to lead the games which he had liked himself . . . only yesterday, wasn't it? Den, head-all, I spy, or (dangerous and for boys only) throwing knives at a target. When the day had gone well, John had his own special reward to offer the children. At the end of the afternoon they put aside their books and sat at ease while he told them stories, with all the drama and imagination which were naturally his. Tales he had thrilled to, of far Arabia, of Washington at Valley Forge, or the savage and exciting stories of Murphy, the Indian Killer. But the frightening tales of Granther Kelly he never told them. Not for children, he decided, and anyway they needed the accompaniment of night, darkness, and leaping fire.

As for the hours outside of school, at first Johnny felt high and dry, unutterably lonely. Then bit by bit the word went round that there was a new young teacher who liked to dance, and one who played a good game of baseball, too, when the fellows let him join.

Into Johnny's notebook, which he kept carefully in these days, crept some rather strange things. A list of girls' names, and dates when he had called on them, one Melissa, two Marys, and others besides. Under "Money I have spent" went charges for hiring a buggy, and side by side with it in the graceful, sloping handwriting went "Item. One new pair of calfskin boots." And always, as a sober note, were included phrases and words which Johnny specially liked, or the title of a book labeled "I must read." And more and more often now would creep in whole paragraphs, experimental openings for some sketch of his own.

At first his lonely longing for Mary Taft was almost more than he could bear. So many things to tell her, so many questions to ask! The one person in all his life with whom he had really shared his needs, the one person he could talk to. Why, she had practically persuaded him to seek his freedom.

Alas, that the only way John took to reach her was just the wrong one! In his desire to learn how to write a good letter he bought a miserable manual from a passing peddler —*The Compleat Letter-writer*. It set a model of stilted,

unreal phrases and absurd politeness, with no place for the warmth and affection which were the genuine Johnny. Poor Mary! Trying in vain to answer, not knowing herself how to translate love into words, she sent back strange little letters which only widened the gulf between them. Bit by bit the notes grew fewer, farther apart. The correspondence stumbled and died.

When summer came and his own schoolyard stood blue with chicory, it seemed to Johnny more than he could bear. For the blue of wild chicory grew along the fence lines and stone walls of the old farm at Roxbury. Now that he was away from the farm, he found that he missed and longed for it. The soft, bright blue of chicory was the color of the sky over Old Clump.

After his first rough encounter with the school bully, Johnny had little trouble with him. Taking time to show the youngster some new wrestling holds, when they were both on the playground, he seemed to have won the lad's grudging respect, and later his friendship. But one of his hangers-on gave him constant trouble. A mean-spirited boy, with crafty underhanded ways, always ready to stir up the other children and goad them into mischief. He came to school in clothes that were threadbare, with great red wrists hanging from sleeves too short and tight.

Much to his disgust, Johnny learned that his next week's lodging was to be in Harry's home, an obligation which it was not proper to refuse. A "boarding-round" teacher must accept what was offered. It was a long walk to the house at the edge of the sprawling village. Even before he entered it, Johnny felt that he understood his pupil better. The poor, unpainted shack, with broken front steps, seemed a proper introduction to the woman who met him at the door. "Come in, Teacher," she said, without smile or further words of welcome, wiping her hands on a greasy apron before she seized one of his. Her son she simply ignored, as if he weren't there at all. A slatternly, straggle-haired woman, with a deep frown between sad and hostile eyes.

Johnny had been spoiled by good warm food at night in most of the homes. People took trouble to "have a chicken for the teacher," or hot biscuits and honey, or a juicy apple pie. In this widow's home the supper was boiled potatoes and salt, with bread and butter on the side, slack-baked bread and "frowy" butter, just the kind his mother despised. Choking it down, he soon found early excuse to be shown to his room. But this, he discovered, was a mistake. The room was airless and hot, set tight against the low roof. The one small window stuck hopelessly when he tried to raise it. Well, fewer mosquitoes, he thought, giving up the struggle. One chair and a sway-backed bed completed the picture. The mattress was lumpy, with deep hollows between the piles of hay. The bed creaked and rocked uncertainly as he climbed into it. But, young and tired, he settled down into sleep.

Then there came a strange and awful dream of falling. Bang, bang, bang! The earth rose up to meet him with terrific impact. Sparks shot out of darkness, the night was filled with fire. A dreadful ache seemed to be all that was left of his head.

Coming to his senses, he put out his hands and felt around

in the darkness. Yes, just as he had guessed, he was flat on the floor. The bed had collapsed, and most of it was on top of him. Slowly extricating himself, he laughed softly. Something novel in beds this, perhaps better than the original! Managing to stretch out a thin blanket, he was soon asleep on the cooler floor.

The next morning at breakfast Johnny's pupil looked at him with malicious eyes. "Thought I heerd a noise in the night. That you, Teacher?"

"*Heard*," said Johnny calmly, helping himself to some jam which was not too bad. "What kind of a noise did you think you heard, Harry?"

The boy's mother turned from the stove to join in the sly questioning. "Hope everything was all right for you last night, sir?"

Johnny smiled and gave them glance for glance. "More than all right, ma'am. I slept the sleep of the just. Now if you'll excuse me, I'd better be starting for school. Coming along, Harry?"

That night at closing time the tall, thin, ungainly boy seemed diffident for once. Shyly he sidled up to the teacher and asked him in a low voice whether he was coming to visit again.

Johnny turned and answered him warmly, "Of course I'm coming, Harry! Coming for the week, isn't it? I'm looking forward to these walks home with you." Just for a moment he laid a hand on the lad's shoulder.

At the painful flush which covered the youngster's face, flowing up to the roots of his brown hair, suddenly John understood. All the pranks, all the mean and underhanded

ways, were the desperate expression of shame and embarrassment and a sense of poverty. Poorer than all the others!
Didn't amount to anything. Well, he'd show them! That
was the way the boy had been thinking and feeling.

From that day on, Johnny took special pains with his
teaching of Harry. By the end of the week, in mother and
son he himself had found two friends.

It was October when Johnny closed the door of his
school and said good-by to the children for the last time.
If he had wanted thanks, the look in their eyes was enough.
One small girl burst into tears and, running forward,
caught his hand, clinging to it as his little sister Adelaide
might have done. "Aw, say, why do you go?" Harry
grunted in disgust.

"Because I'm going back to school myself," John answered, and deep inside was a glow of satisfaction that this
end at least he had accomplished. Fifty dollars saved to
take him on his way to Ashland, the place where now he
could turn student, instead of teacher. For this he had run
away from home—or was he wrong? Was it only for this
he had run away?

At Roxbury John was overwhelmed by his welcome.
Pa wrung his hand and seemed to hate to let it go; Ma gave
him a quick, hard squeeze. Eden capered like a spring lamb,
in spite of the dignity of his teens! In a few days he settled
back into the usual patterns—lugging water, chopping
wood, doing his share of the milking or any other necessary
fall chore. And now he knew that he loved it; loved the
fragrance of the kitchen, the delicious mixture of oak wood

and bayberry candles burning, of juicy pies cooking, luscious with apples, brown sugar, and cinnamon. He loved the family banter, which often he had shrunk from. But no one called him "little idiot" any more.

Most of all he loved the bare, windy pastures and the deep forests of Old Clump, the great stone ledges, high up toward the top, where he had once found phoebes' nests. Now the summer-loving phoebes had flown. Here and there a blue jay flashed through the trees, or an upside-down nuthatch, which Ma called a "devil-down-head," spoke its harsh, warning "hank, hank." He loved the beech woods, the big, bare trunks with the golden leaves below them. He tossed the leaves with his feet and felt the magic of their showering.

In the early dawn of late November Johnny climbed to the high springboard seat beside his father, and behind him the butter tubs creaked as they drove away. At the last moment Ma had rushed forward, a misty figure in the lantern light, to pull a new wool muffler over his head and about his ears. Forever Ma! In the flash of an eye he had become the small boy again, going on his first butter trip to Catskill. But this time he did not jerk the muffler away. Proudly he rode beside his father. Very proudly. For Pa had paid him five dollars for his work on the farm.

Ashland Collegiate Institute was a school just opening in Green County, New York. Johnny was in time for the first exercises of dedication in the new chapel. The sight of two hundred boys and girls about him, the solemn waves of music, the earnest speaking, seemed to sweep him away on a strange tide of exaltation. But it was excitement tinged at first with overtones of fear. How could he find his place here? How would he know what to do, an awkward boy from the back country? Was his training equal to the requirements of this school? What should he choose to study? And how would he find friends from among so many? Once again he was the shy, uncertain boy, not the self-assertive man who had been a teacher.

Because he was eager and hungry to learn, Johnny jumped at all the subjects he could take—geometry, grammar, chemistry, French, physiology, and algebra. The last should be easy, for he'd had it twice already! He added logic, because he didn't know what it was and wanted to find out, and he rose at six in the morning to meet with the logic class in the dimly lighted chapel. Public speaking and composition were both included as a matter of course.

Public speaking proved fun. John Burroughs found his voice and lost the telltale stammer in these five months at Ashland. As for his choice of logic, perhaps it helped toward the love of clear-cut arguments which became part of him.

But now for the first time John's great excitement was writing. At fourteen, in the West Settlement school, he had balked at the themes assigned to him. Who wanted to write about someone else's ideas? The words wouldn't come, or, if they did, they were the wrong ones. He thought with disgust of the time old Oliver had tried to punish him by making him write. Here the ideas were his own and he could ring the changes as he wished. Words— what fun to use words; the longer and more learned they were, the better!

One day, soon after his arrival, the teacher in composition picked up a paper from the top of the pile in front of him. Johnny, sitting in the front row, felt a wave of embarrassment rush over him. Well he knew that familiar writing. Embarrassment? Rather it was an agony of suspense so dreadful as to be pain. Gladly he would have slunk out the door or jumped through the window. Was he to be laughed at before this roomful of strangers?

The teacher was beginning to read. "The last sun of 1854 was gilding the top of the western hills. . . ." On and on the gentle voice continued until the last words were read. Then he put the paper down with a kindly comment. "This work is sensitive and the writing shows promise. If the spelling could be improved now, so that one could recognize the words . . ."

For a moment Johnny hung his head. No, he couldn't spell correctly, even when he had been teaching spelling to others.

To the end of his life he never learned to spell. But the man's words had filled him with a kind of ecstasy. His writing showed "promise"—what could be more exciting than that? Though later he knew, even before he left Ashland, that this effort was hackneyed and immature, perhaps there was significance in the fact that his first sketch was a study of nature, and that its first line mentioned his beloved western hills. When he finally left the Academy, at the close of the spring term, he stood second in composition out of a school of two hundred.

Having to leave was heartbreaking, for again there was no certainty that he could return. He was just beginning, he thought, to get a glimpse of some of the things he needed to know. And now the money was gone. This time Pa came to his rescue, lending him ten whole dollars to pay his way while he went hunting for a teaching job.

Ever since that wonderful day when he had seen his first steamer, he had dreamed of sailing down the Hudson. The apple orchards of Dutchess County were white with their May bloom the day he boarded the great, straining side-wheeler at the wharf in Kingston. He wished he might sail on forever, watching the smooth banks flash by, then change into the wild, majestic shores of the Highlands; watching the white sails tack and turn, like the gulls gliding over them, or the rowboats with flashing oars, or the barges sunk low with loads of brick, coal, and produce for the great city.

Next, leaving the steamer behind him at Jersey City, he boarded a train which would take him to Plainfield, New Jersey. His first ride on a railroad—that, too, was exciting. He wondered before it started whether he would be jerked from his seat, whether he could endure the awful speed of thirty miles an hour.

Now began the wearisome tramping from school to school, looking for an opening, or even for some trustee who knew of an opening. Once he heard of an unfilled post twelve miles away, but when he had walked the distance, he met the familiar refrain: "Sorry, sir, I'm sure we need an older, more experienced man."

He had in his pocket a letter from the head of the Ashland Academy. He had been so sure it would open doors to him! A good letter, he thought.

To Whom it may Concern:

This is to state that John Burroughs is competent to give instruction in the branches usually taught in district schools, and the writer can cordially recommend him as a gentlemanly, earnest, and faithful young man.

Signed,
Principal of the Ashland Collegiate Institute

At first he pulled the letter out and presented it with pride, but at the end, discouraged by constant rejection, he did not even bother to show it. Though he knew he must go home, since his money was fast vanishing, he could not resist the lure of New York City.

As if in a waking dream he wandered about the streets, watching the strange procession of people, the vendors crying their wares, the hackney coaches rolling past, the delivery carts with their bells, or peering at the motley collections of the stores. All the stuff of life, so strange, so unfamiliar, and so fascinating to a boy from the back country.

When he came to the old bookstalls on William Street where secondhand books lay rotting in the sun, at last he felt at home. Lost to time and space he browsed among them, picking up this dusty brown volume, reading at that, completely absorbed and delighted. These *Studies of Nature* by St. Pierre, these he must surely own. Locke's *Essay on Human Understanding,* Samuel Johnson—half a dozen others—he wanted them all. Collecting his prizes into a pile, he took out his small roll of bills and began to count it over.

The owner of the stalls had been keeping a wary eye on this travel-stained youngster with the dirty shoes and the battered hat. He eyed the bills, too, with careful concentration. When Johnny looked up to ask the sum total of his purchase, he found to his amazement that it came to exactly the amount of money he held in his hand.

He must get home. He already had his return ticket for the boat to Kingston. As for food, surely he could do without that. If he saved enough for the coach fare to Dimmick's Corners, there still would be miles to walk, but who minded a little hiking? Sighing, he returned some of the books, with a last wistful glance at the titles. The rest he tumbled into his black oilcloth bag.

As Johnny climbed over the mountain next day, supperless and without breaking his fast, he felt strangely triumphant. True, he had failed to find a school, but this was not a lasting defeat. Heavy on his shoulders was a great prize, more wonderful than all the jewels of which he used to dream. Hours of pleasure and excitement lay ahead . . . visions of glory. *Books!* To John Burroughs they were then, and were always to be, the "keys to the Kingdom."

Chapter 9

IT SEEMED TO JOHN THAT HE LED A DOUBLE LIFE THE summer that he was eighteen. There were the long, hard hours in the hayfield, when he worked shoulder to shoulder with the older men, and there were the coveted hours when he stole away to the woods, to his books and his dreams. He read Johnson's *Idler* and *Rambler*, with his back firm and comfortable against his favorite big rock; Locke in the silence of the beech grove, with only the birds for company. Johnny did not regret his wild extravagance in books, though the boys had laughed at him and Pa had turned red with anger.

He read other things, too. His first novel, *Charlotte Temple*, came by mail. That night, when all the house was asleep, he stole down to the old kitchen and boldly helped himself to one of the rationed tallow dips. Soon he was lost in a new and exciting world, all thought of time and sleep forgotten. In the early light of morning Ma found him there, still dressed, his weary head down upon his arms.

Most often of all he turned to St. Pierre's *Studies of*

Nature, a fascinating, ambitious work by one of the first French naturalists. By what strange chance had he found it, in that dusty bookstall on William Street.

"Plants, it has been said, are mechanical bodies. Well then, try to construct a body so slim, so tender, so fragile as that of a leaf, which shall for whole years resist the winds, the rains, the keenest frost, the most ardent sun. The Pyramids of Egypt are crumbled into powder, but the grasses which clothed the soil subsist to this day."

This book roused John's curiosity and stirred his imagination. It was fortunate for him, in this summer when his interests were growing, that there was no one near him to laugh at his love of books. True, he was a mystery to his family, but he had early learned to discount their judgment. One day when Jane found him trying to write, stooped over his notebook up in the south bedroom, she told him he would surely "hurt his brain"; that "writing was turrible bad for it!" But Johnny only laughed and pinched her till she ran away and left him.

Now the fall was already here, the summer birds leaving, the wind off Old Clump turned cold. John knew that at last he must find that school to teach and no failure could be accepted! New Jersey had rejected him in the spring. Well then, he decided, that was the very place he would hunt again. But once down in the Hudson country, he was tempted to visit Dr. Hull and take one last look at Tongore, where he had done his teaching. Here he was surprised and moved by the warmth of his welcome.

The first man he saw was the old trustee who had originally hired him. "Wal, Johnny," the good farmer

cried, pumping his arm up and down till it seemed likely
to break. "Jest the man we be lookin' fer! You're comin'
back here, ain't you . . . ?"

"Why, sir, I hadn't thought . . . I mean, I am just on
my way . . . I . . ."

At this moment came a charming interruption. A slender, handsome girl bounced into the room, a seventeen-
year-old, he guessed, with sparkling black eyes and the
reddest of full, red lips.

"Oh, Uncle, I didn't know . . ."

"Sulie, let me make you acquainted to Mr. John Burroughs, who used to teach here."

"Delighted, I'm sure," Ursula exclaimed, tossing her
head and showing to advantage her proud and pretty
chin. "I've heard the fellows speak of you!"

From that moment it did not take much urging to con-
vince Johnny that he should teach his school again, at
double the salary, of course, "board and laundry all found."

If he had been lost and lonely when he first came to
Tongore, this winter he felt just the opposite; he hardly
had a moment to himself. What with parties, apple cuts,
and square dances, what with buggy rides, ball games, and
church suppers, the time whizzed by, fast as a good pitch
over the home plate!

No one, he soon discovered, could dance half as well as
Sulie. Many a good measure he trod with her, and there
was no thrill like the feel of his arm about her waist as they
swung through "Hawky Fly Out," or on to the climax
of Grand Promenade.

She was popular, pretty, and self-assured. When she

came into the dance hall there was no questioning the rush of swains in her direction. Johnny found peculiar pride and pleasure in cutting them all out and arriving first. Quite openly she showed her preference. True, she was experienced! There were mysterious hints about "an officer to whom I was engaged," and other chance words dropped which both maddened the young teacher . . . and intrigued him. How could he ever win this proud and haughty charmer . . . if he wished?

By spring he no longer asked the question. She was his girl. He was her declared lover and slave. No hope of marriage yet, for her pa wouldn't hear of it, he knew. There was all his own way to make, and the education he hoped for . . . but . . . ? It was a long, hard *but* for the ambitious, uncertain Johnny.

Let that go for the present. Take the days as they come. Take the joy, and forget the future! Under the dim, high moon of April, Ursula and Johnny went buggy riding down the country lanes. The urgency of spring gave music to the little brooks they passed. From every marsh rang the high, magic bells of the peepers, which Johnny had always loved. How sweet were Sulie's warm, red lips, as his own lingered on them! The reins fell slack on the back of the nag he was driving and the wise "critter" found his own way home.

During the winter John had sent in his application to Cooperstown Seminary and been accepted for the summer term. It was a fine academy, famous throughout the state. Now that the time had come, he found that he could not bear to give up his plans. In spite of Ursula's tantrums and tears, in spite of his own heartache at leaving her, he packed up his clothes and books and went to the school of his choice.

Before he left Tongore, even in the midst of his chaotic love affair, he had managed to snatch an occasional moment for his writing. Disgusted by an article he had read, defending the latest American ism of table tipping and hearing voices from the dead—a craze which was sweeping the country—he had set himself both to answer the article and attack spiritualism. The result, he had mailed to a small New Jersey newspaper, the *Bloomville Mirror*, signing himself "Philomath," since assumed names were the order of the day. But he added his own name and address for good measure. When no answer came back, he tried to forget the matter.

At Cooperstown John began Latin, and he eagerly added the study of English literature. He went on with French and his favorite mathematics. In debating he again made a name for himself.

One day, plunging down the stairs for his mail, he noticed a roll of newsprint sticking out of the small wooden cubicle. Quickly unrolling it, he saw that queer name "Philomath" looking back at him! There, in good black print, served up as a feature article in a well-known newspaper, were the very words which only yesterday had been unborn and shapeless ideas in his own brain. It seemed like a miracle, and all day long he walked on air. It wasn't much, he told himself, trying to reduce his own foolish pride, but he couldn't dismiss the warm, excited glow so easily. *The first time he had ever had anything published.* Not the last, his mind told him.

During the three months at Cooperstown, Johnny's taste in reading changed. At first he tried Emerson and found he "tasted like green apples." He began to dislike the weighty Samuel Johnson and discovered with joy both Wordsworth and Shakespeare. Strange partners! One added to his knowledge of life, the other to his love of nature. At the end of the three months he turned to Emerson again. And now he found that the "Sage of Concord" had a deep and special message for him.

> "He saw the partridge drum in the woods;
> He heard the woodcock's evening hymn;
> He found the tawny thrushes' broods;
> And the shy hawk did wait for him."

That, John thought, might have been written for himself alone, so true it was to his own solitary experience.

Much as Johnny loved his books, there were plenty of other things he liked at Cooperstown. Otsego Lake, a stretch of water set about by evergreens, provided, he discovered, excellent fishing, and there were plenty of fellows who liked to go with him. He longed for Sulie, but . . . well . . . just now she wasn't there!

When he was chosen special orator for the Fourth of July and gave a rousing, patriotic speech outdoors, on the shore of the lake, with all the listening throng around him, how the girls clapped and applauded! For days afterwards they almost ruined him with praise. No doubt Sulie would have tossed her pretty head and cried, she "didn't see what all the fuss was about!"

It was the end of August and the katydids were beginning their dry insistence when Johnny packed his books to leave.

When the big front door clanged behind him at Cooperstown, an important part of Johnny's life was over. Gone forever the carefree days of youth when the future did not press too heavily on mind and heart. What was to lie ahead of him now? What was his path to be? What, his destiny? The boy who "took to larnin' " and who longed to be an author never could go back to school again.

The old saying that the course of true love never did run smooth was a fact for Ursula North and John Burroughs. She was opinionated, sure of herself; he was sensitive and quick-tempered, with a "high flash point." Sometimes he thought wistfully of Mary Taft, who had been so understanding. She had listened to him, had liked to know what a fellow really thought and wanted . . . but he had lost her. How and why he didn't quite know. He had tried to see her again last summer. She was kind and pleasant, but the old warmth was gone.

Ursula was just the opposite of Mary. She liked to do the talking! She told John what he ought to think and do, and she was apt to slap him down when he disagreed. And yet there was a charm in that very assurance— something to lean on! Away from Sulie he could see her faults quite clearly; once with her, he forgot everything in sheer excitement. Perhaps they quarreled because they loved each other so much.

Just as he left Cooperstown, something happened to hurt Johnny. A chance remark in a letter, some bit of gossip—again a wall of resentment stood between them.

At the same time there came a note from one of his old friends at Ashland, a jolly, friendly girl named Cattie Allaben, whose family had moved west. She had written to him off and on ever since.

"Aren't you ever coming out to see us, Johnny?" she wrote. This time she added cannily, "Father says to tell you that out here there are plenty of good schools needing teachers."

"One girl drew me west." That settled it! Deciding that he wanted freer air and a look at another part of the country, he borrowed fifty dollars from Curt (for a wonder he had the money to lend) and left for Illinois.

He liked his little school at Buffalo Grove, near Polo; liked the sense of freedom which the West gave him. He was really off on his own now! Dr. James More, the school trustee, sold him books, among them a Webster's dictionary which he always kept. The people were kind and friendly; he was conveniently near to Chicago. Best of all, a young assistant in the school had a printing press. Now he saw himself in print for the second time.

Cattie Allaben was just as he remembered her, a wisp of a girl, with the freshness of a young willow tree, hair the color of corn silk before the corn was ripe, and big hazel eyes with amber glints in their depths. She had an elfin quality which he loved. At once she greeted him like a long-lost friend, which indeed he was!

"Johnny . . . I'm *so* glad . . . it's about time you came . . . oh, Johnny!"

Every afternoon, when he closed the school door on the last of the children, he took the grass-grown road along

the edge of the wide, tranquil prairie. There in the distance was Dr. Allaben's house, plain to see on the flat land, and beyond it other houses clearly visible, though they might be miles away. Johnny felt the charm of this prairie country, with its grasses standing shoulder-high, bowing and rippling before the strong wind of the West, running to meet the high arch of the sky.

Soon Cattie came swiftly to the door, her hands full of fresh doughnuts or spicy cookies or gingerbread. "I knew you'd be starved, Johnny," she always said. And indeed, she told the truth!

Like children they sat on the front steps and devoured the goodies, or like children they wandered off hand in hand across the level land, watching the wild geese as they darkened the sky, or listening to the boom of the prairie hens or the call of the quail.

But this level land was not his land. Where were Wittenberg, Panther, Cross, and Slide, or, most loved of all, Old Clump? Where were the mountains with their deep, moving shadows, their wraithlike mists, their colors—never the same? Blue, deep purple, or black . . . black in the moonlight. Most of all he missed the mountains.

"And one girl drew me back again." By the next spring the longing for Sulie was more than he could bear. He couldn't forget her. With each week that passed he seemed to miss her more. Cattie was gay and pretty, more a comrade and friend than a sweetheart. No passion in her, no change of mood. But Sulie was a devouring hunger in the blood. Even to fight with her would be a joy!

Coming back through Chicago, Johnny stopped to

have a daguerreotype taken. The face that looked back from it was very young, sensitive, and serious—a fine forehead, deep eyes under level brows, a slightly troubled look. The brown hair was thick and long, as a musician might have worn it.

Even before he went to Roxbury, Johnny stopped at Olive, the little town near Tongore where the Norths had their farm. Ursula would be at church, he knew, since it was Sunday evening. Already the bells had stopped ringing and the church door was closed. Was it too late? Caring little about proper hours of arrival, Johnny crept quietly in, to sink into the first back seat he could find. Eagerly his eyes scanned the congregation. Old ladies, a few men, a scattering of young women and children. Yes, there toward the front was Sulie, demure, with head upraised, her eyes fixed on the young parson. With the detachment of distance and six months away, he studied her. How lovely she was! At that instant she looked around and saw him.

The benediction had not been said and the congregation were still seated when Ursula rose and came down the aisle. Her wide skirts rustled and she marched on proudly, head held high under her cornflower-blue bonnet. Johnny watched her eagerly, though there was a quizzical look in his eyes. What an actress she was! Was she afraid he would escape her again? He followed her out, and the next moment he had forgotten everything but the glad look in her eyes, the warm clasp of her two hands. He couldn't kiss her now, but . . . that was the one thing in the world he wanted to do.

Next day, sitting in the Norths' parlor, Johnny drew

a small box from his pocket and handed it, half shyly, to Sulie. Would she, he wondered, be glad to own his picture, which he had had taken just for her? She seized the gift and opened it eagerly, but Johnny had an instant awareness that his girl was disappointed. She didn't say thank you or even how handsome it was, though that, indeed, she might well have said. Nor did she say that she was happy to have it, or comment on his thoughtfulness in bringing it.

"Oh, Johnny," she cried, "you must have your hair cut right away. In this picture it looks . . . oh, dear, I can't bear to have it long like that!"

For part of another summer John Burroughs returned to the Roxbury farm. But July found him once more with a school of his own, at High Falls, near Kingston, New York. Someway he lived through those first weeks of teaching, his head in the clouds. Then when September came, he broke away for a long week end.

On September 12, 1857, when he was not yet twenty-one, he stood up beside Ursula North to be married by her family minister. His lips felt numb as he said the words, and just once the queer old stammer returned. Her own replies were loud, prompt, and firm. "I do," she answered, for all the room to hear.

A long week end! Rather, a moment without time, which was over like a flash of light. Now happiness and completion and a sense of oneness, shutting out the world. Now the joy of fulfillment in each other's arms. When the two days had ended, John rose in the early dawn of a Monday morning to walk the long miles back to school.

But Ursula clung to him and began to weep bitterly. "You can't go now, Johnny—you belong to me. Who cares what happens to the old school!"

He smoothed back the brown curls rippling over her shoulders, revealed so beautifully by the soft candlelight. For a moment he gentled her and tried to kiss away the tears. "Darling, we knew it would be like this . . . we said so, don't you remember? But I'm the only teacher, and I promised . . . I've got to go."

Again the rain of tears, punctuated by a harsh sobbing.

"Sulie, dearest, please be patient now. Soon as I find a place for you to stay, I'll send for you. I must go, darling!"

Heartbroken that his brief honeymoon should end in such sorrow, Johnny broke away at last and started off. Even when he reached the roadway in the half darkness, his wife's bitter sobbing seemed to follow him.

So Johnny went back to his teaching, and Ursula stayed in her father's home. From the first it was a strange marriage—of a boy without means, or prospect of means, to a girl older than himself, of a proud and thrifty family. It was a marriage of flint and fire, of stone and wind, of earth and running water. Of a woman whose god was material success to a man who had "hitched his wagon to a star" and meant to ride in it. Could it succeed? Would two such different people be happy? As yet the waiting years gave no answer.

Chapter 10

IN THE WEEKS AFTER HIS MARRIAGE, JOHNNY CONTINUED to live in a kind of dream. Forever left behind in the past was the boy who had turned to a "compleat letter-writer" for his inspiration. Now the words he wrote might have fired the pages on which they stood, so filled they were with burning longing and need. No thought of sequence, sentence structure, or even spelling now—only that he needed the love and understanding of his wife, only that he longed above all else to have her with him.

My Ursula:

I am not going to be as formal in my letter as you was in yours; I am not going to call you *my wife*—that sounds too cold and business-like. It is not half so sweet, romantic and lovely to my ear as "my own dear Ursula." I don't feel towards you as men usually feel toward their wives and I can't bear to call you such. My feeling for you has all the passion, devotion and romance of a youthful lover . . . Can we not always be lovers? Will time and care take all of this poetry and romance out of us? . . .

I sometimes think I will not make the kind of husband that will always suit you. If I live, I shall be an author. My life will be one of study. It may be a weakness in me to cherish the thoughts I do, but I can't help it . . . I know I must struggle hard to realize my end, to have my name recorded with the great and good. But if God spares my life, the great world shall know that I am in it . . .

I will try and do as you want me to . . . You may expect me next Friday night if nothing happens . . . So here is a kiss until I come.

Your John

The letter reveals not only love and passion, but also ambition already fixed and set. "If I live, I shall be an author." And added to the touch of youthful bombast is the uncertainty and defensiveness of youth. "It may be a weakness in me to cherish the thoughts I do." In the end comes the pathetic desire to please. "I will try and do as you want me to."

Love and ambition, with a question mark, are revealed in these early letters of John Burroughs. No doubt Ursula answered them warmly and firmly. No doubt she also wrote what later became a fixed saying of hers, that scribbling was a poor business and he'd better give it up.

About a month after his marriage, John Burroughs wrote again.

High Falls, Oct. 7th, '57

My dear Ursula:

I intend to invert the golden rule this time and do

unto others as they do unto me. Your letter to me was
short and business-like, so mine to you shall be short and
business-like. Here is all I have to say at present: I think
I shall probably be up to Olive Friday or Saturday. You
did not ask me to come in your letter, but I want to come
very much, and I hope you will be glad to see me. If I
don't come then I shall be obliged to wait four weeks
and it would be very painful to me to be absent from you
that long. Oh how glad I shall be when you can be with
me all the time!

Adieu. Yours while life lasts,
John Burroughs

The longing for his absent wife, the unhappiness of
living apart from her, which marked this period, was healed
by her coming to live in a boardinghouse with him in the
spring. But not yet in a home of her own, where she could
take pride in her gift for housekeeping, or in the pretty
things which she herself might choose. Shut into one room
in the house of the school trustee, with little that was
real, not even the cooking to occupy her, Ursula became
restless and difficult. And John, busy with his teaching, and
trying in odd moments to work on an article or bit of
verse, seemed far from being the gay companion with
whom she had fallen in love. Worst of all, there was just
no money for any little luxury a woman craved.

"Why in the world can't you give this up, John?" she
asked over and over. "Try for something in business.
You're so clever—you'll surely succeed! We'll just starve
if you keep on schoolteaching!"

Perhaps the walls in the boardinghouse were thin. Per-

haps the trustee and his wife had "long ears" which over-
heard the arguments between John and Sulie. Perhaps
they drew their own conclusions and built a sense of
prejudice against the young couple under their roof.

It was a warm day in spring. The winter term of teaching would soon be over. A new moon tonight, the teacher
thought, as he closed the door and started on the long walk
home. On such a night how wonderful it had been to ride
with Sulie down the country lanes! I'll stop in at one of
the farmers' and hire me a nag, John told himself, and
we'll have a little fun for once. The poor girl's been shut
in too much. It isn't good for her—she's too young.

As he came to the house where they lived, happy at the
thought of pleasure ahead, he noticed the delicious smell
of cooking apples, heavy with sugar and cinnamon, which
he loved. But women's voices drifted out to him, angry
voices raised in bitter dispute—the deep mezzo-soprano of
the trustee's wife against Ursula's shrill, didactic treble.

"Tell you 'tisn't good that way . . . has no flavor."

"Don't see what business it is of yours . . ."

"Keep the skins on. Then the sass is nourishing . . ."

"You ain't the cook in this house. If you don't like my
cooking, you can leave—and good riddance!"

Poor John! He had enjoyed his school and as usual
had won his way with the children. But all that went into
the discard now. When the few days before the end of
term were over, the trustee called him into his office to
say that he would not be wanted again.

"I will try and do as you want me to." For the next
few weeks Johnny patiently pounded the sidewalks of

New York City looking for any business opening he could find. But this was the spring of 1858, a time of uncertainty and unemployment, only a year away from the panic of '57. A time when strange currents of unrest ran through the country like wildfire licking its way through prairie grass. Discouraged and unsuccessful, John returned to his teaching. For the summer term he found a place at Rosendale-on-the-Rondout, and again Ursula returned to her family.

Separation, loneliness, the drudgery of teaching, added to his wife's continuing appeals, made Johnny seek another business venture in the fall. A golden-tongued promoter, who had visited the little village of Rosendale, convinced him of the virtues of a wonderful new buckle, which would make harnessing easy and every farmer happy. Persuaded, because he wished to be, he set about to persuade others. Father North advanced a goodly sum, a kindly doctor in the village contributed a big loan, with glittering promises of more to come, and to this John added all his own meager savings.

For three months John worked in a Jersey foundry at the manufacture and promotion of his buckle, only to find that its patent infringed on another's rights, that it was impossible to market it, that enough promotion money could not be found, and that all his dreams of wealth were the merest mirage. Now he was in debt to his father-in-law and to others also. But again the one sure employment came to his rescue. He was hired by a school in Newark, New Jersey.

This period in Newark was important for one special reason: it was the first time that John and Sulie had been able to have a home. Perhaps the young wife was not over-anxious to leave the safety and comfort of her father's house. But now at last the dominating male asserted himself. Buoyed up by the magnificent salary of one hundred dollars for sixty days, John wrote to his Sulie:

> Get your things to the river, put your clothes in your trunk. Put my clothes in my trunk, together with my manuscripts, Shakespeare's Works, and my two big dictionaries; get aboard the stage; go to Rondout; stay overnight with your cousin; and the next day take the cars for New York and I will meet you at the Depot.
>
> I shall certainly expect you to come, and if you have my happiness and your own at heart, you will let nothing detain you. We can live nicely and happily here. . . .
>
> Our folks are going to send me some apples and butter soon. . . .

And Sulie came. In three small rooms at East Orange the two young people set up their first home. The young wife's real genius for cooking and cleaning and "keeping things nice" had an outlet at last. To Johnny the long walk home from Newark seemed mere child's play, with his own rooftree to welcome him at the end of it.

"Sass" cooked from apples with their skins left on! And Happiness, which is a stew no man can concoct alone.

Something else happened in this winter of 1859 which greatly added to John's pleasure. Starting out one night with the small group of men that formed the East Orange debating team, he soon found himself in a well-packed, smoke-filled hall waiting for a contest with the "doughty men and true" from Newark. For some reason he was in fine form that night and gave his "one, two, three" with vigor. His voice worked well, the words came clearly and swiftly from his lips; he even found the chance to tell a country joke or two, which pleased the house and added to his own sense of adequacy. When the time for the rebuttal came, the opposing team seemed confused, he thought, while his own group were keen and quick at the riposte as an expert dueler's blade. In the end the Orangemen were declared the winners by a number of points.

The rest of the Newark team came up to congratulate them in a crestfallen, perfunctory way, but one slender, attractive man put out his hand to John's with the gayest of smiles. "That was fine debating, Burroughs!" he said. "No wonder we lost. Couldn't hold a candle to it! My name's Allen," he added, "and I hope to have a chance to take you on again!"

"By all means," said John. "Stage a comeback, and put us in our place. How long, by the way, have you lived in Newark?"

That was the beginning of a great friendship, a comradeship between two men with similar ambitions and tastes in common. Allen, John found, was already a freelance writer and lecturer of considerable skill. Gay, witty, the best of storytellers, a devastating mimic, he added a flair for sketching and a love of art to a wide knowledge of books and men. Friends, Johnny had always had—country boys to fool around with, fellow students at Ashland

and Cooperstown. But here for the first time was a man who spoke his own language, who didn't find his "scribbling" foolishness, who even encouraged him with warmth and admiration. For underneath Allen's surface bravado and gaiety was a person both sympathetic and unselfish. Wise enough, too, to see the promise behind the other man's discouragement and despair.

"How about the *Saturday Press*, Johnny? Have you sent anything there? Let me have that bit of verse you just read me. I'll try it on the *New York Independent*."

Again in April of that year, persuaded by his wife and by the nagging burden of debt, Johnny turned to the old, disheartening task of job hunting. From New York he wrote to Ursula, who was visiting "his folks" in Roxbury.

The prospects of a situation of any kind are very poor. The supply of help so much exceeds the demand. They advertised yesterday for twenty men to canvass for the *Brooklyn Register*. I went precisely at the hour, but the room was so full that I could *hardly* get in. I suppose there were near two hundred applied and, as many of them had worked at it before, of course my chance was poor. I shall advertize in the *Tribune* tomorrow.

I know you have an idea that it is a very easy matter to get a place, but your ideas would change if you were to try it a while here in New York. It is the most disheartening business I ever undertook . . .

Well, be a good girl and don't find fault with me

when I do the best I can. You little know my troubles
and anxieties . . .

I wish I could be with you up there among the grassy
fields. I never hungered and thirsted after rest and the
country as I do now.

Days later, still jobless, he reported again.

I let no opportunity slip . . . I have more hope of
getting a place to write than anything else. I sent an
essay to the *Saturday Press* and it came out as one of the
leading articles. I took a copy of verses to the *Independent,* and they said they would publish them.

I bought a hoop skirt for you the other day. I got a
twenty-shilling one for five and sixpence. I knew you
wanted one . . .

In the end the job hunter stood defeated, but his "hunger
and thirst" for the country were satisfied. That summer
young Allen came to visit the farm in Roxbury, cementing
John's friendship for him even tighter. For the language of
wind and mountains and brooks, the joy of long, timeless
days fishing the swift, brown streams, the excitement of a
mountaintop—these too he could share with Allen, as he
had never shared them before with any comrade.

Taking their blankets, frying pan, and knapsacks full
of food, they went off together for a camping and hiking
trip, tracing the Beaver Kill to its source and camping by
Balsam Lake. Together they shared the wonder and beauty
of the night, the mystery of the deep darkness, lit only

by stars. Together they built up the welcome fire, pressing close to its reassuring glow, conscious of primitive unease and dread when a barred owl's triple hunting call sounded behind them, or a fox barked from the mountain. Later John was to write of this experience with words which caught both its beauty and its excitement.

"The friendly and cheering fire, what acquaintance we make with it! We had almost forgotten there was such an element, we had so long known only its dark offspring, heat. Now we see the wild beauty uncaged and note its manner and temper. . . . It carves itself a chimney out of the fluid and houseless air, a friend, a ministering angel in subjection, a fiend, a fury, a monster ready to devour the world if ungoverned. By day it burrows in the ashes and sleeps; at night it comes forth and sits upon its throne of rude logs and rules the camp, a sovereign Queen."

So Allen and John Burroughs became friends, an important and determinative factor in the life of the still unknown young teacher.

1860—year of decision. The slow fires smoldering underground through the vast reaches of cotton and prairie, or New England highlands, now burst into red-hot flame which might destroy a nation.

In a five-to-four decision, the supine justices of the Supreme Court, unduly influenced by collusion with a partisan president (as Seward then maintained) had given the fatal verdict of the Dred Scott case. "No Negro could have any of the rights of a citizen; the Missouri Compromise was unconstitutional; neither Congress nor the

people of a territory had the right to make laws against slavery . . ." But the new party, the Republican party, went on making the prohibition of slavery in the territories part of their platform.

The long-legged, homespun lawyer from Illinois, who only a few years before had sat wistfully before the fire of a country inn, thinking his career forever ended, now sprang forward to his post of leadership. In immortal words he met the "little giant," Douglas, in debate, and almost overnight established his own fame.

"Slavery is the eternal struggle between these two principles—right and wrong—throughout the world. They are the two principles which have stood face to face since the beginning of time and which will ever continue to struggle. The one is the common right of all humanity; the other is the divine right of Kings. Slavery is the spirit that says, 'You work and toil and earn bread and I'll eat it!' No matter in what shape it comes, it is the same tyrannical principle."

An inspired madman seized the arsenal at Harpers Ferry; an emotional woman wrote the dramatic pages of *Uncle Tom's Cabin;* a Kansas torn with civil strife was unable to win acceptance and statehood; a Democrat in the South could not vote with a Democrat in the North, and a new, dynamic party won the dubious glory of the presidency for the courageous lawyer from Illinois.

1860—year of decision.

To Johnny, working on the hayfields of his father's remote farm, all the rumors that shook a nation seemed far away. And yet he had lately seen the streets and offices of New York, talked to lines of men waiting for jobs that never opened, savored himself something of their bitterness, their lack of hope. Much of his own uncertainty seemed a mirror held up to the uncertainty of the country. What was life all about anyway? Was there any future for him? Any opportunity? Or would he sink back into the nameless toil of a farmer?

One thing, at least, he knew that he had to do. Whenever the mood was strongest, or a rainy day came along to give him an excuse, he stole up to the south bedroom and seized upon whatever scraps of paper he could find. He had started an article—it wasn't named yet—but today, with the rain drumming on the roof and shutting out all the glory of the mountains to the south, today he could give his time to words, good words that sometimes did his bidding so well. Today, absorbed and happy, lost in the excitement of his own ideas, he wrote on and on and on.

Later he rewrote his article in his own mind, as he worked at some humdrum job of the farm, taking out one word, putting in another, almost forgetting the task in hand.

Chauncey Burroughs came upon him, standing, rake in hand, completely quiet in the middle of the hayfield, and clapped a fist upon his shoulder with a loud accompanying guffaw. "Woolgatherin', son? Ain't grown up yet, be ye? It's hay the cows eat, you know. . . ."

Old tyrant! Feeling a sudden rush of anger, half inherited from a long ago childhood, Johnny felt also the rising flush of embarrassment. But when he looked up he saw the twinkle in his father's blue eyes.

"Yep, Pa, I'll concentrate on hay for a while!" After all, he was getting paid for his help. He'd better stick to working!

One evening, rounding the corner of the barn, John heard a curious rhythmic pounding coming from the direction of the cow stalls. It was after milking time. What was the meaning of this? Not the hour to be mending or making anything. Inquisitive, he stepped inside, to find Hiram senselessly banging one of the upright stanchions with a broken bit of fence post.

"Hi . . . whatever in the world? What are you doing?"

"Gittin' it out o' my system, I guess!"

"But what's the trouble?"

"Lookit! You git pay fer your work on this farm, but what do I git? Jest nothin'. From mornin' to night I work . . . and jest nothin'! Save Pa money . . . make all the yokes an' sleds an' mend th' harness an' pile the walls . . . an' nothin's the answer. So what do I do?" He raised the broken rail and brought it against the upright with one tremendous wallop.

"Don't do that, Hi!" cried Johnny, deeply troubled. "Why don't you talk to Pa?"

"Won't do no good. I had ought to gone West—long ago."

"Well, don't give up hope. The world is wide!"

Hating himself for his own glibness, Johnny turned away, but he resolved then and there that he'd help his oldest brother, if the time ever came when he could. He glanced back as he went toward the house, to see that Hi had dropped his fence post and was sweeping up the litter about the barn door with long, even strokes. Perhaps he had "gotten it out of his system" . . . at least, for the present.

The article was finished at last, and properly named "Expression." He was pleased with it, there was no denying that.

"Proverbs give us the best lessons in the art of expression . . . they give us pocket editions of the most voluminous truths . . . There is no waste material in a good proverb; it is clear meat, like an egg . . ." That sounded well, he thought. What to do with it was now the problem.

Then John reached a decision. Why not try for the most important magazine in the country, instead of for one that would never help his reputation? It would come back, of course, but then . . . He would send it to the *Atlantic Monthly*. Their list of contributors read like a summary of all the famous and learned. What of it? A fellow could only try. On his next trip to town he stuffed it firmly through the slot under the post-office window. Firmly, because he was afraid he might back down.

James Russell Lowell, editor of the *Atlantic*, seated at his desk in the little Boston office, shoved back the clutter piled high about him with disgust. Now he picked up a huge pile of papers, dumping them unceremoniously into a battered basket, marked "Return to author." Then his hand fell upon a new envelope, which he slit open half savagely. Slowly he began to read. Suddenly he sat up from his slumped and tired posture, braced his elbows on the table, and read on. Well . . . this . . . was . . . different! But it sounded like Emerson. Might be Emerson, of course. But why the name—Burroughs? Never heard of him. And the queer postmark, Roxbury? Was there a Roxbury in New York State, too? Never heard of that, either.

Twisting around in his chair, he put out his hand to a row of books that stood in the case beside him. "The Sage of Concord!" He knew him already, almost by heart, of course.

"Fate," "Power," "Beauty," "Heroism"—he thumbed through the different essays swiftly. Didn't seem to be an "Expression," but the name might have been changed. Frowning deeply, Lowell turned back to the carefully written, gracefully sloping handwriting. If original, this was a discovery, but if not? He was still reading it over when his assistant came in to interrupt him and to urge him out to lunch.

Few letters reached the remote farm of the Burroughs family, but Johnny made an excuse to drop in at the village post office whenever he could get away. Finally, in disgust, he gave up going. Then one day Chauncey Burroughs came back from a trip to the grist mill. When he reached the house, he hauled an envelope out of his pocket. "Who's your friend in Boston, Johnny?" he asked, as he handed over the slim white paper.

John was hardly prepared for the swift and devastating wave of dread that swept over him. Another failure! The thought was an icy hand at his heart. Then he noticed that the envelope was flat and slender; his manuscript couldn't be in that.

"Open it, open it, boy!" his father went on urging. "Tell us the news! We're curious—don't shut us out!"

But Johnny turned away without a word, climbing the stairs to the one place that gave him privacy. For a moment he hesitated, then slit open the envelope to gaze at a single piece of paper, a form letter with print that looked like writing. From the center one freshly written word stared back at him—"Expression."

> Boston, Sept 11th, 1860
> Office of the Atlantic Monthly.
>
> Dear Sir:
>   Your manuscript entitled
>   "Expression"
> has been accepted and will appear in our magazine as soon as we are able to find room for it.
>   Your ob't serv'ts,
>   The Editors

That was all, but, by jiminy, it was enough! He longed to dance and shout and proclaim his news to the world. He longed to burst in upon his family, waving his letter in triumph. They would only think him crazy when they discovered the cause. One forkful of hay, tossed to the top of a hay wagon, would seem more important to them than some silly writing sold to a magazine. He could hear his father laugh and see the wondering pity in his mother's eyes. He loved them . . . he would always love them. But share this with them? No!

For all that, John knew that he had reached a mountain-top. For this he had practiced and struggled; of this he had dreamed. Now the mists were parting. Far below he could see the land fair in the sunshine—*his* country, the country of hope.

Chapter 11

It was a Saturday in fall, at Marlboro on the Hudson. Ursula had been cleaning and dusting every corner of her little new parlor, polishing each article in it with loving care. Now she stood back to survey it proudly. The new lace curtains Ma sent hung stiff and handsome at the windows; from each end of the mantel her china figurines looked charmingly down. The gold velvet cloth with its heavy fringe, which adorned the marble-topped center table, held its Bible at just the proper angle. Would there be writing in it sometime soon, she wondered wistfully, just as her name and Amanda's had been entered in the Bible at home?

Yes, it was a pretty room, in spick-and-span order. Though they had just come here, already she felt at home. Things were looking up! This school was larger and Johnny had said she might perhaps help to teach the youngest children later on. That could be fun, she thought, though she was afraid to try it; children were so rackety nowadays! There was more money, too. John had made twenty-eight dollars from a queer article he had sent to a magazine, and he'd given her some of it, at that.

Ursula took one more long look at her little best parlor; then she went out, closing the door carefully. If the minister or the school trustee should happen to call . . . well, it would be ready, she thought with pride.

Now she heard a stamping on the porch stairs and the front door burst open with a bang. Johnny, his eyes sparkling, his brown hair standing up every which way, his cheeks red from the fall wind, his shoes and clothes covered with dust. Stuck just over one ear, a red fall leaf perched puckishly.

"Grand walk, Sulie," he said, stamping off the dirt from his shoes. "Too bad you don't like walking."

"I've better things to do than wasting my time!" She tossed her head and shook her wide skirts with something like a flounce.

"Well, I've a new idea for an article. Think I'll go in here and get it out of my system. Just about the quietest place in the house." He dropped his hand on the knob of the parlor door and had started to turn it when Sulie was beside him with the speed of an avenging fury.

"No, no, no, Johnny! Not in there—please!"

"Why not?" He looked down at her quizzically. How bright her eyes were when she grew spunky! "Think I'll poison your dear little room? I'll be as quiet as a cheese-eating mouse. Just make a small place on the center table . . ."

"Johnny, no. I've been cleaning it! *No!*"

He was growing annoyed now. After all, who paid the

rent for this house? Who kept the roof over them and the floor under them? But still he held his quick Irish anger in check. "It's my room, too, isn't it, Sulie?"

"I tell you, you're not to scribble in there." The tears were coming; her firm voice rose to shrillness. "I . . . just . . . won't . . . let . . . you." Suddenly she pounced on the key in the lock, turned it, and tore off with it before he could stop her. He saw the gleam of triumph in her eyes.

The floodgates were down now before the white-hot torrent of rage that engulfed him. "Think you've stopped me? I'll . . . just . . . kick . . . your . . . blasted . . . door . . . down!"

With each word he raised a strong, muscular foot and kicked at the paneling till the wood shook, splintered, and fell in. Then he reached through the yawning gap to loose the catch. From behind him, the wild sobs rose into long-drawn wails, but he marched through the shattered entrance, aloof and unnoticing. With one hand he swept the Bible and the velvet under it to the floor and spread his papers out upon the marble top. He had won. He could write in peace now.

But all the ideas which the calm woods had given him, all the hope born of his recent success, seemed to have faded away into a vortex of misery and confusion. Won? He was destroyed! Not a calm or coherent sentence remained in his head. For a long time he gazed at his pages through the churning mist. Then, leaving them as they were, he rushed to the kitchen, seized his gun from the corner, and tore out to the reassurance of the hills.

For many weeks after that Johnny worked at his new piece, "Analogy," sitting on the attic stairs and using the top stair for a desk. Every effort of his mind and heart went into it, he thought, but when he sent it hopefully to the *Atlantic*, it came back without a word of thanks. Perhaps it had been foredoomed from the beginning.

From Allen, his correspondent in the "great world," Johnny learned that everywhere people were discussing "Expression." But since articles in the *Atlantic* had no names attached to them, the idea was general that Emerson had written it.

"So you see, my dear John, the Sage of Concord is reaping your laurels. Shame on the Sage!"

That his own inexperienced work was credited to the greatest name in American letters seemed at first pretty wonderful to John Burroughs. But the more he thought about it, the less he liked it. Was he then only an imitator, parading under a well-worn cloak? Above all, he thought, he must be himself. His writing must express himself or it would never succeed. What did he have to say that a hundred others had not written?

Turning that and other problems over in his mind, he still could not refrain from gloating over his beloved November *Atlantic*. Over and over he read the whole magazine from cover to cover, not omitting "Expression," which, of course, he already knew by heart. In the back part of this number stood a notice of new books; one of them, by a man named Olmstead, was called *A Journey in the Back-country*.

Back country—the name captured Johnny's imagination. Suddenly it seemed a clue, an answer to the problem that bedeviled him. Who, of all the people trying to write today, knew more about the real back country of America than he himself? He began a series, telling about the simple, basic things which his own childhood had met and known —the dog churn, which made the butter come, where sometimes a weary little boy had had to play the part of dog. About wall building and maple-sugar making, that wonderful boiling of the sap in the early spring, when the bluebirds and phoebes were just returning; about these, and other things.

The walls of his own home farm. How often he had gathered stones for them, watched Pa and Hiram building them! In winter, when the snows in the road had been too deep, he had literally walked the walls to school. Now he wrote about them lovingly . . . remembering!

"Not a rod of rail fence, or board fence, except round some temporary inclosures, is to be seen in an hour's walk through the fields, but only dark, high and frowning stone walls cutting the landscape up like a checkerboard and interposing an impassable barrier to all light-footed, ramblingly disposed herds. . . .

"To squirrels generally these stone fences serve as a sort of underground railroad communicating with every orchard, wheatfield, ryefield, cornfield or forest in the whole land, and that by many different routes and without any danger of missing the connections, or having his neck broken by casualties to the train, though, to be sure, he runs a slight risk of being waylaid by a cat, or of being 'peppered' by the fowling piece of some young Hollins. . . ."

Now the words, which often seemed unmanageable in his ambitious, weighty articles, came at his bidding with a

new freedom. "Analogy" had been stiff, he knew, "much like a ring-boned horse." Now it was fun to write. His work seemed simple, vivid, real. It had the freshness of the life he had known. His series, *From the Back Country*, was at once accepted by the *Leader* and since his own name was attached to it, some of the recognition he longed for began to come to him.

It was a cloudless day in the fall of 1861, dedicated to a nutting expedition with Allen, the best of companions. At first they talked of the war, of the disturbing news from Washington; then of the literary world, the motley Bohemians whom Allen seemed to know. Then suddenly Allen pulled a book from his knapsack, a fat, brown volume with *Leaves of Grass* printed in big, sprawling gold letters on the back of it.

"Look, Johnny, I've something new for you. Tell me what you think of it!"

He handed the book over and John examined it carefully. The cover showed an indented picture of the globe —with North and South America rising out of clouds. It was dated 1860-61, and "Year 85 of the States" was added underneath. Published in Boston by Thayer and Eldridge.

"Wait! Let me read you a bit!" urged Allen.

Johnny listened quietly, stretched out on the leaf-covered ground, his back against the firmness of an old beech tree, while Allen's voice began to read.

"The runaway slave came to my house and stopt outside,

I heard his motions crackling the twigs of the woodpile,
Through the swung half-door of the kitchen I saw
him limpsy and weak,
And went where he sat on a log and led him in and
assured him . . .
He staid with me a week before he was recuperated
and pass'd north,
I had him sit next me at table—my fire-lock lean'd
in the corner."

Vivid in John Burroughs' mind, as Allen read, came the
memory of that long-ago day of his childhood when
Granther knelt praying by the side of the old fugitive
slave, to whom later he himself had tried to show the
way. . . .
Turning the pages, Allen continued:

"I am he that walks through the tender and growing
night,
I call to the earth and sea, half-held by the
night. . . ."

Spellbound, bemused, John Burroughs listened, as Allen's vibrant voice read on and on and on. Later he said
that he gained no real idea of the book that day, but that he
felt "held by a tremendous personal force back of the
poetry, a warm, breathing, towering, magnetic presence
that there was no escape from." For the first time, in all his
knowledge of it, he realized "poetry might have the qual-

ity of a magnificent sunrise, or a solitary, dim, old hemlock forest."

The discovery of Whitman there in the sunlit autumn woods was one of the important events of John Burroughs' life.

Marching men, marching men! Sometimes it seemed to Johnny that all the world was on the move, that he alone was static, on the sidelines—useless. Sometimes the sound of tramping feet seemed to creep into his dreams.

After the firing on Fort Sumter, after Lincoln's call for seventy-five thousand volunteers, the long troop trains thundered across the North. Hundreds of "three months men" enlisted to save the Union. Little towns like Roxbury or Marlboro or Olive were gay with bunting and loud with "resolutions." Depots were crowded to bursting. Shy girls, thrilled by their own patriotism, offered food, tobacco, or sweets to young soldiers who leaned gayly from car windows. The soldiers cut off souvenir buttons from their coats to give to the girls.

It was all a game, a picnic, a vast, motley carnival, a secret-society convention, a harlequinade! Few there were in the early days of the war who caught the grim undertones beneath the rhythm of the marching feet.

"We'll put down those Johnny Rebs in a month!"

"We'll hang Jeff Davis to a sour-apple tree!"

Oh long and weary month! Oh bitter tree, bearing the fruit of death!

Soon the overconfident North learned its cruel lesson; learned from the first battle of Bull Run, when its untrained

troops were outgeneraled by the gallantry, skill, and courage of the South. Not to be so easy—this scotching of
Johnny Reb.

A few days after their trip together to the autumn
woods, long letters began to come from Allen in Washington. He had gone there to man his father's army supply
store. It was all stimulating, exciting—and profitable. Why
didn't Johnny come to join him?

> Money can be made, and is being made, selling to
> troops within the lines . . . Dealers in goods are com-
> ing and going all the time. For miles in every direction
> outside the city may be seen the gleam of white tents and
> the flash of bayonets . . .
>
> When I see an opening, I shall exert myself to the
> utmost to have you fill it . . . you must come more in
> contact with men and manners.

Allen's vivid letters added to John Burroughs' growing
restlessness. But the thought of huckstering to the soldiers
did not appeal to him. He had been tricked before into an
alluring business gamble. Not to be burned again by the
same fire, he told himself.

Nor did the thought of enlisting seem too glamorous.
He had never liked to kill even the wild things on his
father's farm, though he had done it often enough from
necessity. An expert shot—yes! But how could he bear to
use that skill against a man exactly like himself? Only different in that he came from the South. He wished to play
his part, he believed in the cause of the North. Like Gran-

ther he abhorred slavery. And the Union must be saved! Torn and uncertain, he still stayed aloof.

After the second battle of Bull Run, with its terrible toll of 14,000 Northerners dead, John Burroughs was even less sure of his decision. Full of dread detail came Allen's account from Washington.

Aug. 31st, 1862

My dear Johnny:

For two or three days there has been a terrific battle raging over the river. The cannon were heard here, and the burning powder smelt. There has been great slaughter. Yesterday the cavalry guards went up to the long lines of hackney coaches in front of the different hotels and made them move to the battlefield to be used for ambulances. The Jehus didn't like it much. They tried to escape by darting up side streets, but horsemen turned them back with drawn sabres. Thousands of civilians are called on to go to the battlefield to help . . .

"Thousands of civilians are called on to help." Johnny reached for his pen and wrote to Ursula, who was away on a visit and ought to be coming home. "It is time that every man shouldered a musket. If you do not come soon, you are likely to find me gone to join the Delaware Blues."

But Ursula came, clinging to him, despairing over him, and the Delaware Blues still lacked their man. By October he had made up his mind. If the war went on (God forbid that it should, but somehow the North must win!) more and more doctors would be needed. He had always been moved by the comfort and help that good **Dr. Hull** could bring. He turned to him now, as long ago he had turned to him in time of need.

Soon he was reading medicine at night in the doctor's office, teaching by day in the little school at Olive. Seventeen dollars a month was all they could pay him, but someway, Johnny decided, it would have to do. Since there was no house to rent, and no rent money, Ursula went home to her father's. But John Burroughs meticulously paid her board bill, though it left him penniless.

Poor, lonely, and depressed, Johnny worked on, coming to his study tired from a day's teaching, finding *Materia Medica* and Gray's *Anatomy* dry as dust and almost meaningless. Night after night he persisted, but the vision he had held of himself serving his country as a competent surgeon seemed to fade away.

One night he sat studying with complete distaste. What did ganglia or tibia mean to him? With a sudden gesture of disgust, he stretched out his arms across the stupid texts, and down went his weary head upon the thin brown sleeves. Then, as he lay so, with the thoughts churning dismally in his mind, from some inner depths, from some strength far below his conscious power to will, came a sense of peace, meaning . . . and hope. It was like the caress of the mountain wind, like the ripple and gleam of a forest brook, like the calm of his beloved beech woods. Pushing away his books and reaching for pen and paper, he began to write.

> "Serene I fold my hands and wait,
>   Nor care for wind, nor tide, nor sea;

I rave no more 'gainst time or fate,
    For lo! my own shall come to me.

I stay my haste, I make delays,
    For what avails this eager pace?
I stand amid the eternal ways
    And what is mine shall know my face."

It was the following spring before John Burroughs published his poem, which he called "Waiting." *Knickerbockers* accepted it, to use in March, 1863. Few people then noticed or responded to it, but when later Whittier chose it for his anthology, *Songs of Three Centuries*, it became known and loved around the world. For to the pain-wracked and distressed it brought, as it did to the man who wrote it, a sense of the dependable rhythm of Nature and of the sure beneficence of fate.

"The stars come nightly to the sky,
    The tidal wave comes to the sea,
Nor time, nor space, nor deep, nor high
    Can keep my own away from me."

Tired of starvation wages, of his own loneliness without Sulie (how good it would seem even to quarrel with her!), and convinced by now that he had no taste for medicine, John moved on to another school. In December, finding a place at Buttermilk Falls, he took it eagerly. This was marvelous highland country; the woods were at his door; West Point Academy with its library was two miles away. Two miles, to Johnny's sturdy legs, meant only round the corner. Best of all, the perfect housekeeper returned, with her gift for making wonderful cakes and pies, cooking delicious meals, keeping a house orderly and neat. How had he ever lived without her pancakes and doughnuts? Temperamental and bossy Ursula might be, but no one could have a greater flair for homemaking.

Spring found Johnny roaming the woods with a new companion, a botanist who taught him the Latin names of flowers and the places where rare specimens could be found. His own natural love of all growing things was roused and stirred by the older man's expert knowledge. Amateur and specialist, each learned from the other, sharing a deep interest in the mysteries of the forest. One thing John could never understand—why there was no light of happiness in Ursula's eyes when he came home from the woods with a gift of yellow lady-slippers, or dogtooth violets.

It was the West Point library which gave to John Burroughs the formative and exciting experience of the spring. Browsing half listlessly among the books one Saturday afternoon, he came across a huge, dusty volume hidden away in a little-used corner. Pulling it out, with his usual curiosity, he found in his hands Audubon's giant folio— *The Birds of America*. He had little of the artist's knowledge of the use of pattern, line, and balance, but the variety and exquisite colors of the birds moved him deeply. Here were the bluebirds he had always loved in all their flashing brilliance, the friendly house wrens building in an old hat, the beautiful wounded gull stretching its dark wing up against a pale sky. Long ago as a child, discovering the strange black-throated blue warbler in the woods, he had vowed to know the birds. Someway the interest had been lost or latent in a hundred conflicting interests. But now the old passionate desire to *know* returned . . . from that time on a new world had opened . . . John Burroughs passed through another door.

All through the winter and spring and early summer, Allen's letters came pouring in from Washington, writing of Walt Whitman and other friends he knew, writing of the excitement and variety of the war. Again he urged John to "stop being a cabbage in the country," to come and join him in "a larger life."

July 4th, 1863

My dear John:

Today amid the sound of martial music . . . I take up my pen to finish my letter to you. I looked out on the Avenue a little while ago and saw a forest of glistening bayonets moving along with sound of drums and bugles' blare and gay colors floating in the morning breeze; long lines of artillery moving heavily along with their light brazen pieces and red trappings, and the rarer sight of a black regiment with burnished arms and glittering shoulder-pieces. To me those even rows of dusky faces, marching with steady tramp, were a great dramatic sight, made more dramatic by the peculiar circumstances. . . .

Walt just passed with his arms full of bottles and lemons, going to some hospital, he said. . . .

July 21st, '63

While Walt and I were beering it the other evening,

I read some of your letters to him, and he was much interested. He sends his compliments and says if you ever come anywhere near him, you must find him out and give him a call.

Walt Whitman . . . and the war. It became an irresistible combination to the restless Johnny. In September he wrote to a new friend, Myron Benton, "I am seriously contemplating going into the Army. . . . I am getting dissatisfied and crave action." But alas for his plans! At this point Ursula became seriously ill. For weeks John was nurse and housekeeper, as well as teacher, faithfully helping his wife until she was well again.

As October wore on, all his sense of frustration, all his longing for change, brought him to a decision nothing could shake. One night he simply closed and locked the door of his school, taking the key back to the school trustee. His days of teaching were over. The next morning he left for the South.

John Burroughs went to Washington in October when "the Southern days had Northern blood in their veins." From the first he was confused, dismayed, and fascinated by the strange, sprawling city, half country lout, half overgrown sophisticate. Pigs and cows still grazed at large on a common where all the world went by. A sudden gust of autumn wind could whip up a cloud of dust from dirty, unpaved streets high enough to blot out the Capitol, but it could not hide the passing ambulances, or the captured Rebels being marched to prison, or the creaking lines of white-covered baggage wagons, or the moving throngs of soldiers in their varied uniforms; it could not hide the shifting kaleidoscope of war.

Johnny twisted and turned on his hard camp cot in the back part of Allen's store. His muscles ached and he woke up with a groan. For a moment, on the edge of consciousness, he wondered where he was. His sleepy eyes gazed up at bars of light thrown across the dingy ceiling by the half-closed shutters. Bars! Then he remembered. No more bars . . . he was free!

Not to wake up to the sound of a complaining voice; not to rush to do household chores; not to hurry off to a demanding school; not to correct children, or papers, or his own thoughtless ways—he was free. For an instant he pulled the blankets back over his shoulders to bask happily in his own sense of leisure; the next, he had thrown them aside and was washing at the small iron sink. No trick to build up a fire in the potbellied stove. No trick for a country boy to cook his own eggs and coffee.

But the first glow of satisfaction was giving way to more sober thoughts. He was sorry that he had left Sulie in a fit of anger. Sorry for the clumsiness with which he had tipped a spider full of grease over on her immaculate floor. No wonder she had scolded him, weak as she was after her long illness! How was she coping with the house and the bills and all the small problems he had left as a trail behind him? He was ashamed, too, of the abrupt desertion of his school. The children had deserved better fare at his hands.

The bills would be paid, he assured himself firmly. A job was the next important thing. He couldn't camp out here indefinitely, taking advantage of Allen's indulgence. As to Sulie, he must write to her and make some things plain—very plain, for once—he told himself savagely.

He brushed his shabby suit carefully, adding a fresh paper collar and cuffs. Fortunate for him they were fashionable nowadays! The sun was still low, and Allen had not come yet to open the store, when Johnny started out. Where should he go, to the Treasury Building or the War Department? He chose the War Department and cooled his heels for hours that day in a crowded outer office. No one seemed free to take his name or speak to him, and the rushing clerks gave him no word or sign. The act of looking through you seemed exalted to a fine art in these Washington offices.

Now and then a man would dash by, carrying an impressive case or roll of documents under his arm, to be greeted at once and ushered to an inner sanctum. Men with no better qualifications than mine, Johnny thought to himself bitterly.

At last at the end of the morning a harried clerk approached him. "Name?" he asked in a listless voice.

"John Burroughs."

"Recommendations?"

"I'm afraid I have none with me."

"Letters of introduction? Some special friend who sent you?"

"Neither," said Johnny, trying to look hopeful.

"I'm sorry, Mr. Burroughs, no use wasting your time here."

The next day, briefed by Allen, John went to seek out

the office of his own member of Congress, the one man, so Allen told him, who could give him the needed introductions. But here he was met by the worst of all possible bad news. His congressman was at home ill, and would probably be on sick leave till the first of the year. January —and this was October! This seemed a stunning blow to the discouraged Johnny.

Coming back that night after a day of futile effort, he passed under the familiar awning of Allen's store, in through its wide-open doors, past its counters heaped with socks, canteens, knapsacks, blankets, war goods of every description, on into the hospitable little back room which was his one place of refuge.

There stood Allen, waving his arms while he held forth with his usual bravado to a dozen young hangers-on, grouped round the familiar stove. Tipping back in a camp chair, an older man sat with them, listening with a look of infinite good nature and acceptance to the young cockerels about him. A wide-brimmed gray hat sat on the back of a mass of shaggy gray hair; his shirt was open at the throat, showing a hairy chest; a pair of long gray-trousered legs were stretched across a neighboring stool.

"Johnny, thank heavens you've come! Let me make you acquainted with . . . Walt Whitman."

Even before the words left Allen's lips, John recognized the older man sitting so casually with the group before him and knew that here was the one person he had come to Washington to see. Knew it by the excitement in his veins, by the queer constriction in his throat, knew it by the sudden breathlessness which made it hard to speak. Why was he always so backward when something important was at stake?

But Walt Whitman ignored the silence and understood the shyness. Without rising, he stretched out a large, firm hand, engulfing John's and pulling him forward. A pair of wide-set blue eyes looked up into his with a kind of burning intensity. A rich, mellow voice cried out, "So here you are, young fellow! Allen's been reading me some of your letters. Sit down beside me . . . you and I are going to be friends!"

After weeks of waiting a job did materialize in the Quartermaster General's Department at Geeseboro Point, a strange job for the sensitive, bookish schoolteacher. At first he superintended supplies for the Cavalry, giving out drugs, keeping tally on hay loads. The farm boy put the schoolteacher in his place and he did the job willingly and well. Then he was put in charge of the burial of Negro soldiers. To the end of his days he never forgot the long, rigid rows, the twisted black faces. They tortured his sleep and lived on in his memory.

Asking for a different task, he was transferred to an office, sometimes kept very busy, sometimes hanging around in boredom. He brought a book with him to work now, or his current favorite, the *Westminster Review*. One day an assistant quartermaster came in for inspection. Other clerks gave great show of industry, but Johnny was lost to the world, buried in the yellow pages of his magazine. The next day came his dismissal.

The day of his discharge John wandered the streets in

loneliness and despair, hating to return and tell the news to
Allen, hating to see Walt's pitying eyes. Kindness was the
one thing he couldn't bear now. Trying to put on a jaunty
air of self-assurance, he wandered into the Hotel Willard.
He had often found sanctuary of a sort in the smoke-
wreathed reception room. Had even tried a bit of "scribbling" there, when his nagging troubles would leave his
mind. He was working on a bird article—he hoped for the
Atlantic. But today his ideas were static; the peace of the
woods could not be reached. There was no entrance to the
stores of memory, no key to the garden.

Pulling a piece of notepaper out from the drawer of the
desk, he began to write.

November 24th, 1863

My dear Ursula:

I am writing to you much depressed and disheartened.
I have lost my place and know not what I shall do next.
. . . I wish I had not left the Falls. . . .

Nothing has gone with me in this world as I thought
it would. My life is a failure. I have nothing but *ideas* and
do not see that I can ever bring them to bear. If you
were well, you need not want, whatever might become
of me; but you are out of health, and I out of employment. The Lord only knows what will become of us!

A few days after his dismissal, John saw the big, pic-
turesque figure of Walt Whitman in the distance, walking
under the trees on the public grounds north of the White
House. He pressed eagerly toward him, wondering at the

haversack hanging from his shoulders, at the shapeless, bulging pockets and hands full of bundles.

"How are you, my boy? Just going to the hospital to give the men a little fun. Want to carry these bags of fruit for me and come along?"

The big shedlike ward of Armory Hospital was crowded with rows of cots thrust close together, with hardly a space between; on the floor, on thin pallets, other men lay stretched, waiting their turn for some bed that the grim hand of the Reaper might make free. The groans of the suffering, the low complaints of the dying, the stench of sickness swept toward them as they entered. For a moment John wavered, sensing a revolting giddiness. Then he followed Walt, who moved on between the beds with the kindly, casual air of one who felt at home.

In the distance a youngster propped himself suddenly on one elbow and shouted, "Hi, Walt, gimme my 'baccy!"

The next moment a clay pipe was thrust between his lips and the big man stooped to scratch a match.

Thin, clawlike hands were filled with oranges or raisins or apples; yellow faces turned to smile, and eyes glittering with fever looked up into a face alight with compassion and pity.

"How's Charlestown today?" said Walt gently, touching the shoulder of a young Southerner. "Want me to finish that letter home? This time I brought an envelope and stamp."

Skillfully he bent to catch the stumbling phrases, and soon the word was ready to send, a simple human message that would bridge the hatred, the bitter chasm between South and North.

At one bed he paused long and silently, looking down at the rapid breathing, at the young head twisting from side to side convulsively. He smoothed a big, quiet hand over the boy's hot forehead and for a moment the twisting ceased.

"Want me to read a bit from the Book again?"

There was no answer except the merest sign—the lifting and dropping of one tired hand.

"The Lord is my shepherd, I shall not want. . . ." On and on to the end of the triumphant old psalm Walt Whitman read, in a voice that was slow, gentle, and deep. When he touched the boy's pulse at the end, he murmured quietly as if to himself, "Asleep at last . . . and at peace." When he turned from the bed, John saw that his eyes were filled with unshed tears.

From this time on, John Burroughs felt that he knew Walt Whitman. No criticism of the press, no contempt from the literary peers of the day, could shake his estimate of him.

"Walt is glorious," he wrote to Ursula. "I love him very much. The more I see and talk with him, the greater he becomes to me."

Chapter 12

John Burroughs sat on the edge of his camp cot staring into the darkness of Allen's deserted store. Beside him burned the thin flame of one kerosene lamp, which served, it seemed, only to make the shadows deeper. The gay voices, the banter, the arguments of Allen's young friends had faded away. Now he was left alone with his own thoughts; now his own past seemed to take form and shape; rose . . . to stare back at him.

He was jobless, baffled and uncertain of the future, and yet he knew, with a determination nothing could shake, the kind of future he wanted. To be an author—yes, that was still the most important thing in the world. But did he have something real to say, something that was his own, not merely the echo of a greater voice? Could he ever learn to say it?

Often in hours like this he was tempted to throw everything to the winds and enlist at once. God knows the Army needed him! But he had no illusions about soldiering. He had seen the men driven along the roads, herded like animals in open carts; he had seen the hospitals with their bitter aftermath of battle.

Most of all he longed for the peace and quiet of his own home, with a loving wife to help him. Yes, he longed for Sulie. And yet it was easier to be away from her. Only the other day he had written her in complete sincerity, "It is better for us to be apart."

For six years they had lived a turbulent married life, with separations, quarrels, lack of money, and illness to plague them. Worst of all, the life he wanted meant nothing to Sulie. Writing was "scribbling," and "scribbling" in hours after his teaching was only selfishness, since it took the time he should have shared with her. Perhaps, he thought wistfully, if there were children? Would her harshness be softened? Would happiness come to them both? Better no children, he reminded himself, than those whom a father could not provide for!

As he stared into the darkness, firmly he took stock of the past—and the future. In his heart of hearts he couldn't really blame his wife. She had been a proud, handsome, ambitious girl when he married her. She had seen some brilliance or promise in him . . . so she had often told him. It was not her fault that their standards were different, that the kind of success he wanted meant only failure to her. Not her fault—but was it his?

What future lay ahead of them? If he found a job, should he send for her? Or tell her clearly that this was the end? At any rate, let there be an end to hedging and quibbling between them. He would write to her plainly—tomorrow— as he had decided a hundred times before. Blowing out the light, he lay down on his hard cot, softened only by army blankets. Now, battered by his own thoughts, he tumbled and twisted himself into sleep.

In these difficult days, it was the companionship of Walt Whitman that did most to save John Burroughs. At forty-four there was little of heartbreak, frustration, and broken hopes that Walt himself had not known. His *Leaves of Grass*, though greeted with joy by a few, had been despised, rejected, and misunderstood by most of the leading writers and reviewers. His *Drum Taps* could not find a publisher. But he seemed to meet life with cheerful acceptance, giving himself and his limited funds to the service of the hospitals; haunting the wards with whatever gifts he could bring.

Walt, like Johnny, loved to take to the open road with a long, swinging stride, loved to share the stillness of the woods. Sometimes they rambled along Rock Creek, or up Piney Branch; sometimes they followed the old Marlboro Road off beyond Georgetown and on to Cabin Johns. Or they met for lunch in town at Harvey's Restaurant, to have an orgy of eating oysters. Sometimes they walked at night under the trees north of the White House, looking up at the branches, stark and black against the moon. The meaning of the soul, whether there was, or could be, a life after death—anything and everything the two men discussed. Sometimes the finer companionship of silence stood between them.

Long afterwards John Burroughs said, "I loved him as I never loved any man . . . I owe more to him than to any other man in the world. He brooded me; he gave me things

to think of; he taught me generosity, breadth and an all-embracing charity. He was a tremendous force in my life. It was really Walt that drew me to Washington—through Allen's letters."

The trying days crawled past. Christmas came and went, and still Johnny's Member of Congress had not returned. But at last on January 8th an excited, cheerful, and happy letter went off to the distant Sulie.

My M. C. returned Monday . . . Tuesday I got two letters of recommendation from him, one to the Secretary of War, and one to the Comptroller of the Currency. On Wednesday I went up to the War Department. After waiting nearly three hours I was unable to get an audience, so I rushed out desperately, saying that I would not crawl on my belly to them. With hardly any hope I took my letter into the office of Hugh Mc-Culloch, Comptroller of the Currency. I saw he was a very kind looking man, so felt encouraged at once . . . After considerable conversation, he told me to come up next day . . . Today at nine I commenced and worked till four registering letters . . . I do not expect to be able to sleep for a week, I am so glad! My salary will be not less than $1200. a year.

Now at last Johnny plucked up courage to write a letter to Sulie which was somewhat in the nature of an ultimatum.

I see plainly that there is but one way we can live together again as we ought, and that is this; you must take me and love me and be satisfied with me just as I am, with all my faults and imperfections, or with all my coarseness and wickedness if you choose to call it such. This is the only possible way under heaven whereby we can live in peace and love. If the good in me does not counterbalance the bad, in your estimation, then of course you cannot love me. I cannot sacrifice myself, or what is the same, my tastes, my pursuits, my ideas to anybody.

I have much confidence in myself . . . I see my way clearly . . . If you can take me as I am, and when you can't approve, say nothing, things would go smooth enough. Only let me alone and give me love.

I should be much happier to have you with me, if you can come in the right frame of mind, and keep that old promise . . . to take me "for better or for worse." You remember also that you promised in the self-same moment to "love and obey" me, but I will ask only the former . . .

Write me by return mail.

For days after this drastic letter went off to Ursula, Johnny regretted it and wished it back. Had he destroyed when he meant to heal? Would it be the end between them? He was haunted by the memories of early happiness and a fresh longing for the wife he really loved. Eagerly he looked for mail, and when at last a thin envelope came back to him, he tore it open with hands that trembled. Had the self-assured Sulie decided that his words showed only a passing mood? At any rate, she ignored them and sent a mere word or two about . . . nothing. She needed money. There were more bills to be paid. She was "turning" an old dress. She had been making apple butter . . . Desperate and bitter, Johnny tore up the thin sheet and thrust it into the ashes of Allen's old stove.

That night, by himself in the lonely store, sleep would not come. For hours, it seemed, he stared into the darkness, hearing the klop-klop of passing hoofs or the rattle of sabres, as an army troop went by. At last, rousing himself, he lighted the dim lamp, seized writing tablet and quill, and hunted for the words he needed.

At first he wrote swiftly and heedlessly.

> You need expect no more long letters from me, if you can repay me with only a stingy little sheet, part full. I am sure you have time enough to write . . . If you have nothing more to say on the subjects I wrote about, no confessions or promises to make, then, of course, keep silent. I can alter and change myself only as you alter and change toward me. I am not to blame if you are no companion for me; you must make yourself such . . .

Then, as he wrote, a picture of Sulie came back to him—thin and pale from illness. He saw her big sad eyes, her lovely rippling hair. He remembered the courage with which she had tried to do her work . . . and go on. Who was he to condemn her? Now he wrote more kindly, thinking of her, too.

> I know you have had a hard time of it with me, and

with your sickness and loneliness. I see plainly what you have suffered, poor child!

If you had had the love of Nature and of books that I have, I see you would have been much happier.

But as he sat on the edge of his camp cot, stooped over his tablet, Johnny felt again his own loneliness and misery. A touch of self-pity came back to him, and the scratching quill translated it into words.

Now, with a prospect of worldly success, I seem poorer than ever. If fortune favors my purse, but starves my heart, I have but little to be thankful for.

Complaining, he told himself now, would never make Sulie understand. She would despise it as weakness. Could he find the words to make her see the difference between them? Could he add to understanding, not block it? For a long moment he hesitated; wrote; scratched out a line— and wrote again. He must tell the truth, let come what would. He wrote on.

If you have ever thought of such things, you know there are two kinds of success; one is . . . seen and known of men—such as getting a fortune, fame, friends, position . . . This is the only success the world knows or strives for, and I fear it is the kind of success you think most of, as it is for failing in this that you have blamed me most . . .

But . . . I see clearly that the only kind of success

worth having is inward, virtual, unseen; the gaining of wisdom, the understanding of the Universe, the seeing beauty and meaning in everything God has made.

I will send you money fast as I get it. If I stay here, I should expect to go home next summer, and could then stop and see you. *Choose for yourself,* and may you have health and peace and love, whatever happens to me.

Ever yours,
John

What Ursula chose was quickly shown by Johnny's letter of February 18th.

I am rejoiced at the prospect of seeing you so soon. I hope your health may keep good so that we may not be disappointed . . . I will be at the Depot when the train comes in.

The soft, early spring of Washington, with the sky a clear, blue dome, fairer than the dome of the Capitol. In the deep, wooded nooks of Piney Branch John and Walt found the liverwort and the bloodroot pushing up their buds, the shy trailing arbutus hiding under its leaves. "The bluebird's note came down from the air overhead, like the first tremulous voice of Spring," so John Burroughs wrote in his notebook.

True to his word, he was waiting at the depot when Sulie's train came in. He saw the slight, proud figure coming down the steps, one hand holding tight a big yellow basket. Suddenly her set face was illumined by a flashing, happy smile, and he knew by the warmth at his heart how much he cared. Almost gayly she came toward him.

"Look, Johnny," she cried, after he had kissed her, "I've brought you a whole basketful of my own preserves!"

Like the melting snow of winter, the tensions, fear, and distrust of John and Ursula seemed to vanish away. Once again the experiment in love and understanding was renewed; once again they found happiness in each other's arms.

John Burroughs' new job was to act as guard over millions of banknotes placed under lock and key in the big vault of the Treasury Building. In the northwest corner of the second floor, he sat on a high mahogany stool at a tall mahogany desk, facing the great expanse of an iron door, which no one could enter or leave without his personal knowledge. Briefs of letters must be made, registered, and filed; packets of unsigned notes must be put away; outgoing packets, which the banks had called for, must first be counted and registered before they could be taken.

United States Treasury Clerk First Class—the lowest of all available classifications, long hours, stale air, confinement—a strange job for the freedom-loving Johnny. But after all, it meant money in the pocket, steady employment, happiness for Sulie, promise for the future. What if there were occasional empty moments which a fellow might snatch for his own? What if there were writing on the desk, which did not deal with banking or accounts?

It was the *iron door*, John Burroughs often said in later years, which acted as the entrance to a world he longed for. In protest against that ugly wall of iron, he "unpacked the memories of the farm boy he had been," setting his imagination free to follow the mountain streams, to climb the long, rolling slopes of Old Clump, to listen to the clear call of the hermit thrush drifting down from the hemlocks.

Before he left his last little school, he had started an article on the birds; again in the distress and uncertainty of the past unhappy weeks he had struggled to go on with it, first in Allen's store, and later at the Hotel Willard. Had struggled in vain. Someway, the magic was gone. But now, clear and plain, the call of the hermit seemed to sound in that close and ugly room, and he tried to turn the pattern of its music into words. What did it say? Could he catch the clarity, the solemn joy of it?

"O, holy, holy! O, purity, purity! O, clear away, clear away! O, clear up, clear up! Silvery, silvery, so fine, so fine!"

With his inward ear he seemed to hear it sing, now in a high, now in a low key.

But the birds of the imagination yielded in joyousness to the birds of the real world. Springtime in Washington— the woodsy smell of earth, fresh from a passing thunder shower; long, drooping tassels on the silver poplars, a veery singing near the White House, the "rich whistle of the fox sparrow on the Smithsonian grounds, clear as in the Deacon woods at home." Sun warm on the back by day, and in the evening, Sulie to walk with in the moonlight!

One afternoon, coming from work, Johnny stooped to pick an enormous golden dandelion growing in the plot

of grass before the Treasury Building. He brought it home
to Sulie, saying that at first he thought it was a golden
eagle which Secretary Chase had dropped, but decided that
"a greater hand than Chase's had planted it!"

Sulie laughed and tucked the weed into the edge of her
blue basque, where it made a pretty contrast, John thought
—the blue and the gold.

Washington was still a country town, set in the midst
of a wide expanse of wild land. Ten minutes' walk, and
Johnny could reach the woods. In his birthday month—
April—he wrote happily to Myron Benton, "My favorite
flycatchers are here," and reported, too, that he had seen
the titmouse, purple finch, robin, bluebird, wren, song
sparrow, phoebes—and butterflies, he added as an afterthought.

There were other signs and symbols less lovely in that
critical spring of 1864, for Washington was the heart of a
nation and that nation was at war. Dread and sorrow . . .
but also hope; for Grant, the bulldog fighter, had been
moved from the West to be the new commander of the
Eastern armies. Grant would overwhelm and press back
Lee's ragged troops. On to Richmond would be a reality—
this time.

It was still spring when Walt and Johnny stood on the
corner opposite the Willard Hotel to watch Burnside's
army flowing through the streets. All day long the endless rows of glittering sabres, the gleaming rifle barrels, the
Stars and Stripes waving, the quick, heady music of the
fife and drum. Ten thousand Negroes marching proudly,
conscious that the eyes of the world were on them, conscious of a strange destiny.

The offices had emptied themselves upon the streets that day. People waved and shouted with hope and expectation, and Johnny, mercurial and sensitive, was swept away by the pomp and glory, by the enthusiasm of the crowd. But Walt, standing beside John, watched with a set face and saddened eyes. Here and there a soldier turned to wave to him, his face lighting up as he recognized the broad shoulders and wide-brimmed hat of the man who had cared for him when he lay in the hospital. "Walt . . . Walt!" another shouted. Now a boy broke ranks, seized Walt Whitman by the arm, pulled him along beside the marching men. For a moment he kept step, then fell out and returned to John.

All day long the flowing ranks—all day long. And few there were who thought or knew that day that soon in the desperate battle of the Wilderness, in that holocaust of the dark and gloomy woods, a third of the gallant marchers would lie dead.

In these days John Burroughs, as he glanced from his window in the Treasury Building, sometimes saw the President stepping over piles of lumber with his long, lank legs, as he took a roundabout, unwatched route to call on Secretary Seward. Walt Whitman saw him, as he passed on his way to or from the Soldiers' Home outside the city, where he stayed in summer to avoid the heat. Saw the rusty, tall, black silk hat above the tanned face, marked with weary furrows; saw the plain two-horse barouche and the cavalrymen riding about it with sabres drawn.

It seemed to Whitman that the President noted him. At any rate, it was his proud boast to "Jack," as he called John Burroughs, that he had bowed to Lincoln and Abe had returned the bow. But John, who was often amused by signs of Walt's self-conceit, answered shrewdly, "He nods automatically to the people on the streets, Walt, but he looks to me to be lost in thought, withdrawn from the world."

"Perhaps," Walt admitted.

The spring of promise stretched out into a summer of despair, a hot, dry, insufferable summer. Defeat after defeat met Grant's well-trained men, for Lee's ragged troops fought with incredible gallantry and courage, his officers with leadership and finesse. The weeks went by. Grant was no nearer Richmond than McClellan had been.

The awful carnage turned all Washington into a hospital. Ambulances—hearses—steamers on the Potomac, bringing in the dead. The enthusiasm of the North changed into bitter resentment. Abuse was heaped upon the head of Lincoln; he was blamed for "putting a butcher" in command. This was the lowest ebb tide of the war.

Then came the early days of July and the terrifying news of a defeat just beyond Baltimore. On the edge of the Monacacy River, General Early's Rebels had turned the tide of the Sixth Corps, Rickett's division under Grant. The way to Washington was open—or wasn't it? The railroad line was broken. No mail, no messages by telegraph. Terror and uncertainty held Washington in the grip of hysteria, the Capital that was defended now by only a few "hundred-day men," a veterans' corps, some dismounted cavalry, a small, imperfectly trained local militia. Already the refugees were pouring into the city, carrying great loads on their backs or huddled in carts. They reported that the country was "overrun by gray-backs." Secretary Stanton told Lincoln not to ride out to the Soldiers' Home that night.

John Burroughs, seated at his high desk in the Treasury Building on the eleventh of July, heard through the open windows, a distant rumble that was not thunder. For weeks now he had been drilling with a group of other clerks in a vacant lot, wearing a blue uniform which at least looked military. The time had come, he told himself, to break this pose of detachment. With quick decision, he closed the ledgers on his desk, appointed a clerk to his place, and went out to hunt up Allen.

He found him presiding over a store which was swarming with frightened men and women. Pushing through the mob, he persuaded him to go out to Fort Stevens, as soon as the darkness fell, when they might stand some chance of eluding the pickets, or escaping the marauding Grays.

Nightfall found the two men pushing along Seventh Street, but soon they separated since Allen insisted they should follow the road, and John that their only chance was to skirt the fields. With caution he skulked along the edge of the woods, now in, now out of the trees, with all the farm boy's sure instinct, the hunter's cunning. Several times he glimpsed, or thought he glimpsed, a shadowy picket, but stumbled on, managing to flank them.

He was coming closer to the fort now—a line of rifle fire gave him the direction—when a rough voice came out of the very air beside him. "Halt! Who goes there? Give the countersign!"

A countersign could not be manufactured or invented. Throwing himself on the mercy of the blue-coat, he tried a touch of the old blarney, arguing that he was on his way to join the defense, had come without arms to prove his innocence, wished to add his skill to the slim quota of troops. In the end, the man grunted and let him go, growling out, "Lucky fer you, feller, I didn't plug you!"

Through the long hours of the night Johnny crouched in a rifle pit with the veterans of the Sixth Corps, who hailed him with good-natured derision, thrust a rifle in his hands, and laughed as he squatted quickly when a bullet whined beside him. The roar of the guns was loud now, the flashes on the horizon vivid and constant; constant, too, the soft thud of the Minie bullets around them.

Now a shadowy form stood on the parapet. Short, curt orders barked out crisply. The man beside Johnny, and the man beyond, stood up to be marched away into the darkness, volunteers for an advance attack. And suddenly the pit of John's stomach retched with a deadly nausea. This was soldiering. This was what it was like.

All his old terror of the dark returned to him, the sickly fears which Granther had bequeathed to him with his tales of horror. But still he held his ground, hands clamped tight on the rifle butt, waiting . . . waiting. When would the Rebel attack come, or would a Union charge forestall it? God help him, if an attack did start, to prove himself a man! Tense and strained, his limbs cramped and rigid, he waited—hour on hour.

Then at last he saw in the sky the first faint streaks of light. Deciding, with a desperate restlessness, that the long night was over and that no attack would come, he climbed out of the rifle pit and flattened himself upon the ground. The good feel of the earth. The relief of cramped muscles, freed at last. For a long time he lay there; then, seeing in the distance a line of lights, he crawled toward it, moving intermittently and with caution.

The low, trainlike shed was, as he guessed it might be, a frontline hospital. Here, at least, he might be able to be of use—real use, instead of posing as an unskilled murderer. The operating tables were full. Men lay on the floor, twisting and groaning, or leaned against the walls in stoical endurance. In a distant corner lay piled a grotesque mass of arms, feet, hands.

Trying to stifle down the wave of horror that broke over him, he found himself beside one of the surgeons, holding the bloody vessels, handing instruments, trying to be cool and helpful. Walt, he kept telling himself, as the stench and horror seemed gaining on his self-control, Walt would be calm, efficient, thinking of the men, not of himself. Walt . . . But suddenly the room began to swing around him; a terrible vertigo rushed over and held him in its sickly power; and through the churning mist he heard the voice of the surgeon crying, "Get-out-fast-you're-no-good-to-us-now."

Gasping for breath, clutching the ground, again he lay stretched flat along the restoring earth. "No good to us now." No good—as a soldier. No good—as an aid to the wounded. No good, no good. How long did he lie there in remorse and despair, hearing the whine of bullets in the darkness? Ashamed of his weakness, sick in body, mind, and heart, he climbed at last to his feet and went back through the woods to Washington.

Chapter 13

ON THE NIGHT OF JULY 12, THOUGH JOHN BURROUGHS did not stay to witness it, the gray-backs took to flight after a sudden charge from Grant's men. But General Early managed to slip his forces away under cover of the darkness. Not till October was Washington really safe from the threat of the marauders. Then the brilliant Irishman, Phil Sheridan, made his courageous ride to Cedar Creek and turned defeat into victory.

After Early's raid the hot, dry summer dragged on in uncertainty and gloom. As election time neared, an undercover cabal worked against the renomination of Lincoln. "And a man's foes shall be those of his own household."

But the long dirge of the summer ended in the crescendo of triumph. Victory after victory—Farragut at Mobile Bay . . . Sherman at Atlanta—changed the mood of the North and kept Lincoln in the Presidency.

Again it was John Burroughs' birthday and the edge of April, the month he loved. Seated on his high stool facing the iron door of the vault, he heard a new noise coming from the street below him. This time, not the sound of

guns, but a great booming roar, like the pounding of angry
breakers on a beach, driven before the storm. Leaving his
office guarded, he rushed to the door to find himself caught
and carried along by a hurrying throng of workers.

Again the offices emptied themselves on the streets to
join in the mad rejoicing. Strangers wept and embraced
each other; men leapt in the air, shouting and waving.
Newsboys yelled themselves hoarse. Bells tolled with the
quick, sharp note of triumph, to the accompaniment of
whistles from the Potomac. For Richmond had fallen.
The long war was at an end. Six days later Lee surrendered
under the apple tree by Appomattox Court House.

The early spring of '65 found John and Ursula living
in a quaint brick house on Capitol Hill. A good acre of
land went with the house, and a Negro man of all work,
named Drewer, who belonged with the place and came
complete with a horse and wagon. Though the combination was only rented, Sulie cared for it as if it were her
own.

Here Johnny found himself scratching the back of the
ground, driving away the "blue devils" with a bit of honest
toil. Even better than play of the imagination was the
good, familiar feel of earth on his hands, and the sight of
his own vegetables pricking up in even rows.

Here Whitman came for breakfast on Sunday morn-
ings, always late, to Sulie's despair. Precise and prompt
as she was, the coffee had boiled over, the pancakes grown
soggy and cold by the time the big, easygoing Walt arrived. But he sauntered in with such a glow of pleasure
and assurance, such praise for her "wonderful food,"

that John's quick-tempered wife never dared complain. Though she was "all in a pucker," she just cooked breakfast over again.

Then there were the walks and the long, involved talks as "Jack" and Walt went out for their Sunday stroll—sometimes to the woods, sometimes across the common or along the streets of Washington. For to Walt, "lover of populous pavements" that he was, the ever-changing panorama of the streets was strangely satisfying. As the two men passed the white picket fence around the White House, Whitman always stopped to fish for a talisman he kept hidden in one of the fence posts—a smooth round stone. As they walked and talked, he tossed it from hand to hand, and when at the end of the stroll they returned, he thrust it carefully back into its hiding place.

In the evening, when supper was over, and the soft air sometimes lured them out together again, Walt and Johnny wandered under the trees, looking up at the brilliant springtime stars. For several nights that April they noticed Venus, the evening star, which hung low like a great lamp in the sky, so bright and big it seemed like some strange, incredible portent.

It was the morning of the fifteenth of April. John and Sulie were waiting for breakfast in their little house on Capitol Hill, John restlessly pacing the front parlor and Sulie watching her breakfast cooking, or glancing anxiously out the window. Where in the world was Bridget anyway? No milk for the cereal, no cream for the coffee. John would be late at the office, something he abhorred. Should she send Drewer to look for Bridget? Impossible! He would only disappear himself.

But at last came the stamping of heavy brogues on the steps and the old milk woman bustled in, rattling her cans. Her very presence showed sorrow and distress as she blurted out, "The saints preserve us, Ma'am. I'm not to blame for the hour. The President is shot—they do say he is dying, Ma'am! I couldn't get past the soldiers . . ."

"Bridget . . . are you sure it's the truth? God forbid!"

John stood beside them now, gazing at the two women in shocked amazement. The next instant he had rushed out the door.

He returned soon, carrying the morning paper and a number of extras. Sitting at the breakfast table, with their food untouched before them, he and Sulie read them silently with set and troubled faces.

Extra!
President Lincoln Assassinated!
He Was Shot in the Head at Ford's Theater.
Escape of the Assassin
Attempted Assassination of Secretary Seward
Intense Excitement

Last evening at about 9.30 P.M. at Ford's theater the President, while sitting in his private box with Mrs. Lincoln, Mrs. Harris, and Mrs. Washburne, was shot by an assassin who entered the box and approached behind the President. The assassin then escaped upon the stage, brandishing a large knife and made his escape in the rear of the theater. The ball entered the back of the President's head. The wound is mortal.

1.15 A.M. The President is still alive, but is past recovery. He remains insensible and his condition is utterly hopeless.

The Vice-President has been to see him, but all company, except members of the Cabinet and the family is rigidly excluded. Large crowds still continue in the streets, as near to the house as the line of guards will allow.

                                        War Department
                                   4.10 A.M. the 15th

To Major General Dix:
    The President continues insensible and is sinking. Secretary Seward's wounds are not dangerous. . . .
                            E. M. Stanton,
                            Sec. of War

To Major General Dix:
    Abraham Lincoln died this morning at 20 minutes after 7 o'clock.
                            E. M. Stanton,
                            Sec. of War

To the end of his days, John Burroughs never forgot that morning—the deep sense of shock and grief, the throngs on the streets, silent, orderly, sorrowing, the soldiers controlling them with drawn swords. His own garden, fresh in its first green—new life vivid and lovely in a time of death. And over and through it all, the constant tolling of the bells—the long mournful tolling, tolling . . . for Abraham Lincoln, who had saved the nation, but could not watch its slow rebirth.

"*With malice toward none,* with charity for all, with firmness in the right, as God gives us to see the right, let us strive on to finish the work we are in; to bind up the nation's wounds; to care for him who shall have borne the battle."

Strange mystery of fate—that the great leader could not "strive on to finish the work." But that, John Burroughs thought, is the legacy he has left to all of us.

Through many weeks, John had watched Walt Whitman's poems on the war changing and growing. Walt called them "Drum Taps," and often, as the two men sauntered together, John had seen him stop suddenly to fish in his pocket for a scrap of paper, to record some new idea which had just come to him. Or, "How does this go, Jack?" he would cry eagerly, reading aloud a bit of something new.

At the time of Lincoln's death, Walt was away in Brooklyn, trying once more to arrange for the publication of his material. It was in the course of printing when the shooting occurred, and at that time there was no poem on Lincoln included. But when he returned to Washington, he told John Burroughs that he was working on a tribute to the great martyr President, one poem especially, perhaps more than one.

"Jack," he said, his usually cheerful face solemn with grief, "Lincoln is particularly my man—particularly belongs to me; yes, and by the same token, I am Lincoln's man; I guess I particularly belong to him; we are rooted in the same ground."

"True," John answered slowly, not antagonized by the

seeming conceit, but understanding its meaning. "There is a deep kinship between you."

"I am writing a dirge, a lament for Lincoln," Walt continued, "and I need your help, Jack! I am using three symbols. First—the lilacs. They were heavy with sweetness the day he died—the bush in my yard in Brooklyn—heavy with life and sweetness. And—do you remember the evening star so low in the sky?"

"Of course!" John answered.

"But I need a third symbol. What is the name of a bird whose song is solemn, not gay—some bird, not of the open fields, but of the lonely places?"

"Do you know the hermit thrush," asked John, "the shy, brown bird with the loveliest voice of all the thrushes?"

"Describe him to me!" said Walt.

So John Burroughs made his contribution to one of the greatest of all Walt Whitman's poems, called at first "President Lincoln's Burial Hymn," but later always known by its first line.

"When lilacs last in the dooryard bloom'd—
    And the great star early droop'd in the western sky in
        the night,
    I mourn'd, and yet shall mourn with ever-returning
        spring.
    Ever-returning spring, trinity sure to me you bring,
    Lilac blooming perennial and drooping star in the
        west,
    And thought of him I love.

. . .

In the swamp in secluded recesses,
A shy and hidden bird is warbling a song.
Solitary the thrush,
The hermit withdrawn to himself, avoiding the settle-
　ments,
Sings by himself a song.
Song of the bleeding throat,
Death's outlet song of life, (for well, dear brother,
　I know,
If thou wast not granted to sing thou wouldst surely
　die.)　　. . .

For the sweetest, wisest soul of all my days and lands—
　and this for his dear sake,
Lilac and star and bird twined with the chant of my
　soul,
There in the fragrant pines and the cedars dusk and
　dim."

In spite of the shadow cast by the death of Lincoln,
June of 1865 was a good time for John and Ursula. The
Atlantic had published "With the Birds" as a feature article
that spring, and now the mail was excitingly full of letters,
of praise, congratulations—or criticism.

Sulie was kept well occupied and contented at last by
the demands of her Washington home. She approved of
the garden and began keeping chickens, as any good farmer's daughter should. She brooded over them more than the
hen herself, John said. As for Drewer, he was ecstatic when

he could bring in to the "Missus" a fresh clutch of eggs.

Through the long, dull days, facing the iron door, John thought of the hours ahead of him when he could turn the good brown earth in his little garden. He hurried home early to catch the precious moments of light, for the boy who had once tried to run away from hoeing or digging or raking had become a man to whom they seemed necessary and life-giving. He worked hard on the even rows of cabbages, carrots, and beans, and was proud when the passers-by stopped to admire them over the white picket fence.

If the spring of '65 was a happy, domestic time for Ursula and John, for their friend Walt Whitman it was a time of heartbreak and bitterness. In addition to his long hours at the hospitals, Walt had held for six months a clerkship in the Indian Bureau of the Department of the Interior, not well paid, but earning enough to support himself, send some much-needed money home to his mother, and buy many of the gifts which he took to "my wounded boys."

On the thirtieth of June came an unexpected change. Reporting for work as usual, he found on his desk a single official piece of paper.

> Department of the Interior,
> Washington, D. C. June 30, 1865
> The services of Walter Whitman of New York, as a clerk in the Indian Office, will be dispensed with from and after this date.
>
> James Harlan,
> Secretary of the Interior

To Walt Whitman this was a devastating blow. He had done his work well, he felt. There had been no complaints; in fact, he had been promoted once. But now no appeal was allowed, no hearing possible. Without legal advice, without knowledge of the charge, without any further security, he was dropped from the roll of the bureau and given the stigma of failure.

But if Walt was poor in money and security, he was rich in the devotion of the few friends who knew him well. William O'Connor of the Lighthouse Board, John Burroughs, Charles Eldridge (his former publisher) soon found the cause of his mysterious dismissal. Someone had tattled to Secretary Harlan that the quiet, self-respecting clerk in his department had written an evil book, called *Leaves of Grass*.

The fat was in the fire then. Secretary Harlan, at a time when Walt was absent, had ransacked his desk, so the story ran. There he had found—and carried off— a slender book covered in blue wrappers. Dipping into it, without understanding, and without a complete reading, he had decided that the gossip was true. The author of *Leaves of Grass* was an undesirable person.

To John Burroughs, this insult to his friend seemed incredible. What could he do to help? No stone must be left unturned.

"If *Leaves of Grass* is immoral," he said to Ursula, "then so is the Bible, Homer, Shakespeare—most of the great books of the world."

But Sulie shook her curls in skepticism. "Oh, I like your friend Walt, and all that, Johnny, but I do hear he writes some very peculiar things!"

Devastated at this injustice to Whitman, his friends began to make what appeals they could, to pull all available wires. It was William O'Connor, the brilliant, energetic Irishman who had helped Walt earlier when he came penniless to Washington, who managed to pull the right one.

Though Walt had a new job and all the freedom he needed in his work, his sense of shock and injustice continued to rankle.

John Burroughs, too, could not put the injustice to his friend out of his mind, or fail to be moved by the contempt for and misunderstanding of the poems, which seemed to him little short of great. He knew, of course, what many of the reviewers had said of them. There was that horrible review in the *Boston Intelligencer* which had called the *Leaves* "a mass of bombast, egotism, vulgarity and nonsense." Even Emerson, who had once written to Walt with enthusiasm, "I greet you on the threshold of a great career," now spoke of him as "half song-thrush, half alligator," and seemed to have grown cold in his support. Something must be done. It was time to speak out with convincing words and forthright pen for the man who so much needed defenders. Seizing every leisure moment at the office, and writing far into the night, John managed to finish an article on Whitman which he sent to *The Galaxy*. At first the editors sent it back, then wrote again, saying they would accept it. It came out at last in December of '66. This was the first article ever published in America about Walt Whitman.

Walt was delighted. Walt was so childishly pleased that

he wrote to his mother to have "Jeff or George get the magazine for her," adding, "It has a piece about me—I think it is very good."

While John was working on his analysis of *Drum Taps,* he wrote to his friend Benton that he hoped to expand it into a book. He thought it had all the points he needed, and he would soon develop it further. For weeks he mulled over and worked over his book of criticism, *Notes on Walt Whitman as Poet and Person.*

At last the book appeared—half of the copies in rust-brown jackets, about the color of a thrasher's back, half in the dark green of an old pine tree. Now that the book—his first book—was out, Johnny viewed it proudly . . . and wistfully. Success, or failure, he wondered, as authors have always wondered since the beginning of books. Would anyone notice it, care for it, review it? Would it make any difference? Most important of all, would it make any difference for Walt? Help to turn the tide of prejudice in his favor? Perhaps! He could only wait to see.

He had begun it modestly with "First Acquaintance," which told how he had grown up as a farm boy, wise in the ways of the outdoor life. "I loved a few books much, but I loved Nature . . . with a love passing all the books of the world." He went on to say how he had first met *Leaves of Grass,* having it read to him in a sunlit autumn woods.

Through the first part of his book Burroughs viewed *Leaves of Grass* from every critical angle, walking around it carefully, analyzing and comparing. This section was divided into seven parts, filled with frequent quotations from the *Leaves* themselves. Part two of the *Notes* was a personal sketch of Whitman, the man, and ended with a review of *Drum Taps*.

"The great truth that the men in the ranks were the real heroes of the War—that they bore the heat and burden and won the prize—is the marrow of the poems. Above all, he sings the lost. . . ."

It was August when John Burroughs wrote a trifle sadly to Benton that his book "had not excited much comment as yet." What little there was "had been better than he expected!" But alas for John's high hopes and courageous plans! When the reviewers had been given their copies—too often ignored—and Walt had taken a generous number, the rest stood in green and rust-colored piles in a corner of Sulie's sitting room.

Each day she flicked her dustcloth down the pyramid of books, sometimes chanting maliciously, "Poet and Person," with undue emphasis on the *person*. One more proof she thought, that Walt was mildly demented and Johnny, as usual, wrong.

But John Burroughs accepted stoically the indifference to the first book he had ever written, and the first book ever published about Whitman. Sometime, he told himself, it may turn out to be in demand. It had not been easy to write—and it had taken courage to write it. More than anything else in the world he longed for a literary career, but by backing Walt, the most controversial figure of his time, he had offended the very men who might make his own career possible. What of it? John Burroughs, in complete, boyish enthusiasm, never once regretted his choice.

Perhaps he did not have a taste for soldiering, or the endurance of a successful surgeon; but, although it never occurred to him to think of it, he had his own kind of courage—plus out-and-out, complete loyalty to a friend.

Through these months in Washington, John Burroughs was saving money; or, at least, his wife, due to her thrift and careful management, was saving it for him. After their years of hardship and poverty, to tuck away one hundred dollars a month seemed to them the height of worldly wealth. Soon they were talking of building, and not long after that their very own home was rising brick by brick. It was a ten-room house on V street, on the northern edge of Washington. One end of the house faced the fields and woods; the other turned a reluctant face to the city, much as its owner did.

With what pleasure John laid out his big new garden, planting his fruit trees, shrubs, and vegetables! With what pleasure and devotion Sulie scrubbed, polished, and kept her new house in order! "Even the cat has to wipe her feet on the mat now, before she comes in," John told Walt, partly as a warning, and partly as a confession of his own secret dismay. Such rigorous housekeeping always disturbed him. In his heart of hearts he thought it a form of tyranny.

But these were good months for John—good months that stretched themselves out into good, creative years. More and more nature articles began to come from his pen, such as "Snow Walkers" or "In the Hemlocks." Camping and hiking in the summer vacations gave him new experiences and a fresh outlook, out of which grew "Birch Browsings," "Speckled Trout," and "A Bed of Boughs."

It was the turn of the year in '69 when he wrote to his devoted Benton:

> The *Atlantic* gave me $250.00 for three articles. *Galaxy* has an article of mine which I shall look for in the next number. I have another bird article partly finished, which I shall send to Lippincott. Do you know what they pay?

Just as John's book on Walt Whitman had grown slowly from his article on *Drum Taps*, so now out of these various essays slowly developed the plan for *Wake-Robin*, that first charming nature book, which was to make John Burroughs famous overnight.

Carefully he rewrote, edited, cut, or expanded his original material, altering words or changing titles. The old essay, "With the Birds," became now "The Return of the Birds," and formed the first for a book of ten chapters.

"In the Hemlocks" gave a description of the song of the hermit thrush, which he had patterned so long ago from memory as he faced the iron door; gave it in terms of his own hearing and response to it.

"A few nights ago I ascended a mountain to see the world by moonlight, and when near the summit, the hermit commenced his evening hymn a few rods from me. Listening to this strain on the lone mountain, with the full moon just rounded from the horizon, the pomp of your cities and the price of your civilization seemed trivial and cheap."

"The Invitation," as he named his last chapter, returned again to that experience of his childhood, when he saw the wonderful, unknown bird in the Deacon woods.

"Years ago when quite a youth, I was rambling in the woods one Sunday with my brothers, gathering black birch, wintergreens, etc., when, as we reclined upon the ground, gazing vaguely up into the trees, I caught sight of a bird that paused a moment on a branch above me, the like of which I had never before seen or heard of. It was probably the blue-backed warbler, as I have since found this to be a common bird in these woods; but to my young fancy it seemed like some fairy bird, so curiously marked was it and so new and unexpected. I saw it a moment as the flickering leaves parted, noted the white spot on its wing, and it was gone. How the thought of it clung to me afterward! It was a revelation! It was the first intimation I had had that the woods we knew so well held birds that we knew not at all. Were our eyes and ears so dull then?"

When John's book was finished, he turned to Walt for a title, as long ago Walt had asked his help with a poem.

"What shall I name it, Walt?"

It was Whitman's proud boast—though he loved a bit of exaggeration—that he thought of thirty titles for Jack's new book.

Wake-Robin was, as a title, a bit of a mystery to readers

who did not know the wild flowers, had not met the lovely nodding white trillium growing on the floor of the forest. But even more than the arbutus, even more than the hepatica, wake-robin was the very symbol of spring to those who knew and loved it.

The book wore its title proudly, for it, too, held the loveliness, the freshness, the pure magic of spring. All over the country it was greeted with enthusiastic praise, from small-town journal to leading metropolitan magazine. William Dean Howells in the *Atlantic* said: "The dusk and cool and quiet of the forest seem to wrap the reader. It is a sort of summer vacation to turn its pages. . . . It is in every way an uncommon book that he has given us, fresh, wholesome, sweet, and full of a gentle and thoughtful spirit."

But perhaps best of all, there finally came to John Burroughs praise from the great American naturalist, Elliott Coues: "Your book has been to me a green spot in the wilderness, where I have lingered with rare pleasure. . . . I have learned from you, too. The golden-crowned thrush never sang to me as he has to you. When the grass finch spoke to me, I did not understand. . . . I never read thrush music entirely aright before, nor had the least idea where the Canadian warbler built his nest."

Throughout America, hundreds of readers could have written these same words: "The golden-crowned thrush never sang to me as he has to you." But strangely enough, as they met the magnetic beauty of John Burroughs' pages, they not only shared the experience of the writer, but resolved then and there that such an experience must be theirs, too. What they gained was not merely a passing pleasure, but the feeling that they wished to find a new way of life.

John Burroughs had discovered the medium that was rightfully his. Through desolate years of frustration, misunderstanding, and failure, he had clung with devotion to one difficult resolve: "If I live, I shall be an author." "More than one kind of success," he had written to Ursula. The kind he wanted—and worked for—had come to him at last. Now he was sure of his path. Clear in the light stretched the beckoning road before him.

Part Three

1865-1921

Having studied the mocking bird's tones
And the flight of the mountain hawk;
And having listened to the incomparable one,
The hermit thrush in the swamp cedars
Singing solitary in the West,
I strike up for a new World.

WALT WHITMAN

Chapter 14

JOHN BURROUGHS' LIFE AT THIS TIME SEEMED TO HAVE
settled into a curious ten-year pattern. For about ten years
he taught in country schools, unknown and poor, but
always with an inner ambition and strength which carried him forward. Then at the end of the ten years, he
closed the door of his last little school with abrupt and
final decision.

Now almost ten years of his life had been given to the
Treasury Department at Washington. He had begun as
Keeper of the Vault, but ended the period as Chief of the
Organization Division of the Bureau—a reliable officer,
quietly efficient, completely trusted. In 1871 he had been
sent to England to convey fifteen millions in United States
bonds, and to supervise the tearing up of old ones.

One more year he lingered in Washington, taking time
to write four delightful articles on his October abroad;
then with a firmness of decision equal to his earlier one,
he knew that he could "eat government dirt" no longer.
In Washington it was not the ledgers and figures, not the
management of bookkeepers and clerks, not even the shift-

ing political scene, which had interested him. His real pleasure came from the hours spent up Piney Branch with Walt or O'Connor, or turning the good brown soil with his hoe in the garden on V Street. For John Burroughs, like Antaeus, giant wrestler of the old Greek fable, must touch the earth to feel himself renewed and strong. He knew now that he was a countryman, first, last, and foremost, that what he wanted more than anything else was to live on and by the land.

On and by the land! Yes, but was there something else? All his life he had been hoping, searching, fighting his way toward freedom. He was still a boy when he had broken away from a loving but too repressive family. Through the lean years of teaching and the demanding years in Washington, he had still struggled to claim the few—all too few—moments when he could be himself. To find time to write; to question and learn the secrets of nature; to translate the answers into the words he loved— this, and oh, more than this! Where and how could he find this greater freedom, the very meaning of life itself?

Now came the joy of looking for the place he longed for, at first on Long Island, Walt's old country, then along the Hudson where the towering blue Catskills seemed to welcome him. When he found the farm near Esopus, eighty miles above New York City on the west shore of the river, he knew that his search was ended.

The nine-acre Deyo place was a lovely stretch of land, sweeping down over long, rolling meadows from the highway at the top to the very bank of the broad, shining Hudson. The slope of the ground was southeasterly, open for hours to the warmth of the good morning sun. What a place to grow fruit trees, berries, grapes, or vegetables! What a place in which to wrest one's living from the soil!

John had always loved the changing moods of the great river, though a small mountain stream was even closer to his heart. He knew that here was a highway for the birds, a pathway for all the migrations; that without leaving this place the wealth of other lands would come to him. "A jay would bring the woods; the gulls and the fish hawks would bring the sea; the wild swan would bring Labrador and a loon on the river would bring the Canadian lakes."

But even as he meditated on studying the birds, his practical farmer's eye noted a big stone heap on the land, stuff for building right at hand. He already knew that his house would be stone, with gable ends of stained brown wood—a solid house without pretense or sham, the kind of house that represented himself. One other thought brought him to a decision. Over the distant blue hills lay Roxbury. The old boyhood farm, which he had once left with such eagerness, now seemed the place where he longed most to be. Beside the Hudson, and not too far from Roxbury—yes, this was the land to choose. This would be home.

Happily he wrote to Ursula, who had stayed behind to show the house on V Street to buyers, and to wind up all the details of their Washington life:

> I could make a very pretty place of this in a few years. I have made a plan of our house and made the house itself in pasteboard. It has taken me three days to

build it. It looks very nice. . . . If we could reduce our-
selves to the size of mice, we could go to keeping house
in it right off. Tell me all about things, and *feed my
trout.*

Later, with wistful foresight, he added:

If we were not alone I should not hesitate about this
Deyo place, but the great bane of my life has been
loneliness. We two are not enough in a house. . . .
What shall we do? Can we make it up by dogs and cats,
and a pig and a horse, a cow, hens, etc.?

But John Burroughs was not yet rid of Uncle Sam
and his Treasury Department. Though he had resigned as
clerk, he was appointed receiver of a bankrupt bank in
Middletown, New York, and spent weeks straightening
out its tangled finances. Later he was made National Bank
Examiner for districts along the Hudson, for other places
in New York State, even in the South. This meant money
in the pocket, no doubt useful to help pay for the stone
house which was slowly growing on the acres by the
Hudson, all through the hot summer months of 1873.

Back and forth he commuted between Middletown and
the river, keeping an eagle eye on the masons, helping
to choose and place the stones, even invading Roxbury
to find the good Catskill ash, maple, cherry, or butternut,
and to give a hand in cutting and hauling the wood. No
work too difficult, no wood too hard to find for his beloved new home.

With amazement, almost with awe, the workmen looked upon their boss, who seemed to "smell out stones" by instinct. They did not know that this slender, bookish-looking man had been trained in childhood by the rigorous discipline of mountain-country wall building. "Good as six men," the Scotch mason declared, "and hondy," he added, with an admiring shake of the head.

Stone by stone and panel by panel the house grew. The next spring, after the work began, a cheerful letter went off to the much-missed Walt:

> I spend all my time at work about the place and like it much. I run over to Middletown to look after bank affairs for a day or two, then back here. The house is being plastered and will be finished during the summer. The wrens and robins and phoebe birds have already taken possession . . . and if they are allowed to go on with their building, I must stop mine. During that snow-storm the last of April, the hermit thrush took refuge in it. We are surrounded with birds here and they are a great comfort and delight to me. Your room is ready for you, and your breakfast plate warmed. When will you come?

"I spend all my time at work about the place." For two years John Burroughs was busy—simply living. No time now for quiet sauntering, no time to "chew his literary cud." And yet, since everything he did seemed grist to his mill, later one of the loveliest chapters in his books grew out of these days.

What to call the place now that it was done? Rock Ribs—or some other name? No place is complete until it has been christened. But at last Riverby was the descriptive title.

Riverby-on-the-Hudson became forever associated with the name John Burroughs. And the sturdy stone house, with the Norway spruces at its door, still stands today. Though it has known the touch of fire and the hand of time, it remains a memorial to the man who built it so lovingly and well, with due thought for the integrity of the wood and the beauty of the stone.

John's first days in his beautiful new home on the river were joyous ones, delightful because of what he had gained, and because of what he had escaped. No more rigid office discipline, no more time clock; he could breathe again! It had been years since he had sat facing the iron door of the vault, but that iron door still seemed a symbol of the Treasury Department. He had left it forever. To be sure, banking problems still followed him, but he could attend to them in the hours he himself chose, using his own judgment. Each new day was a fresh adventure now; each morning he woke up wondering what exciting discovery he might make.

It was the thirteenth of May and all Riverby seemed a garden, set against the sparkling blue river. The peach trees were full of bloom and the "golden thighs" of the bees passed in and out of them in steady procession. Long before Ursula had thought of her coffee pot, John was up and out, wandering, observing, exploring.

Now he crossed the road above the house and plunged

into the moist tangle of the woods. His eyes, quick as an Indian's, noticed a "lively little shadow on the ground in front of him," cast by an object above and behind him. Turning quickly, he noted the cause of it—a "redstart, performing its astonishing gymnastics in a leafless oak tree." Now high, now low, it flashed about the tree, with drooping wings and outspread tail, the very embodiment of motion. So swiftly it moved, the whole tree seemed to be "festooned by a black and orange cord." But watch as he might, and keen as his sight was, he could not detect one of the insects the brilliant little warbler was catching. "The game it took was certainly invisible."

Coming back at last, John found Sulie impatiently waiting for him. "If you'd ever remember, Johnny, what time it is! 'Tisn't as if you had anything to keep you . . ."

"Oh, yes, I know!" he answered wearily.

This was one aspect of freedom he had not gained, he thought; would he ever gain it? Already at Riverby a rigid housekeeping discipline had been established, a bogus set of hours, it seemed to John, which must never be questioned. For that would be heresy! It never occurred to Sulie that she was master of her time, and not its slave.

Early enough she had pointed out to him that the beautiful stone house was badly planned for housekeeping. Too much "up and down." A basement kitchen and dining room; library and parlor above that; bedrooms on the third floor. It was just climb, climb, climb—either up or down!

"Get a maid to help you, Sulie," he had begged. "Ask Emma to give you five days a week."

"But she won't come."

And wouldn't stay if she did, John thought to himself.

After breakfast, looking for peace, he turned into his own study, which now seemed too dark and gloomy. Why had he not placed it on the river side, where all the morning sun would have streamed into it through his windows? But that location had been given to Ursula's chill and formal parlor, the pride of her heart, and always kept closed. For a moment he picked up his latest book and glanced at it again—*Winter Sunshine*, begun in Washington but published since the building of Riverby. Stuck between its pages was a letter from the famous Boston publisher, James T. Fields, the man who brought to fame most of the great writers known to his day, from Whittier to Hawthorne. John still had a momentary thrill when he saw the note.

> When an author sends out a book like *Winter Sunshine* to charm and instruct the whole country, somebody ought to thank him heartily for a service done to America. . . . I wish to be among the first to say what enjoyment you have given personally to
> Cordially yours,
> James T. Fields

But publisher or no publisher, John's mind was soon back again with the lively redstart which he had found with such joy in the oak tree. Should he start another bird article, while the memory of it was vivid? Not just now, he told himself. Then another idea came to him.

All his life he had kept notebooks, almost from the

time he was a child. Into them had gone everything, from country dance calls to his own early attempts to answer the riddles of the universe. But these notes had been infrequent. Now he suddenly decided he would keep a real journal, consecutive and conscientiously held to. What could be a better beginning for it than the sight of a spring warbler?

May 13th, 1876. "Standing in the road over in the woods, I saw a lively little shadow. . . ."

From an account of this particular warbler, John wrote quickly on to describe warblers in general.

"Each species of warbler, it seems, has its own range and prey. The insects this redstart took certainly could not have been taken by any other bird. In the lower branches and bushes, the black-throated blue warbler was pursuing its game very leisurely, picking it up at rest, and never taking it on the wing. About the orchards and open trees I saw the blue yellow-back probing the flowers and buds with its beak, either for honey, or else a microscopical insect. The creeping warbler was scouring the trunk and branches for its food, not forcing a way to it, like the woodpeckers, or probing deeply like a brown creeper, but picking it up, apparently on the surface of the bark and lichens. The ground warblers find their food on lone plants and shrubs. The Kentucky warbler is often on the ground, picking off worms or insects from the undersides of low, overhanging leaves."

So John Burroughs started his *Journals* with a minute and careful description of the warblers, facts which he had learned from loving and constant observation, in a day without bird books, lists, or published guides. Later, when he was called the "Sherlock Holmes of the birds," nothing could prove more fully than his *Journals* how much he deserved the name.

Down through the years they became the record of his joys and sorrows, successes and defeats—no incident too small, no occasion too great to be included, from the diving of a fish hawk in the river, to the moment when Yale University gave to the man who never went to college the degree of LL.D. ("A fine affair, but hot, hot in my swallowtail!") Most of all, the *Journals* give an intimate picture of the heart and soul of a great naturalist and a great American.

"The bane of my life has been loneliness." John had written this to Ursula when he hesitated about buying the place on the Hudson, so quiet, remote, and different from the teeming life of Washington. And he had added, "We two are not enough in a house." Part of Sulie's difficulties, he knew, came from the fact that she was too much alone.

He had always regretted that they had no children, remembering now with wistfulness his own days in a big family. Forgotten were the tensions, heartaches, arguments, and disappointments he had known; cherished in memory were the nights around the great fireplace with Granther telling stories, or the apple cuts, dances, and quilting bees—all the lively fun of a big group. One of the reasons he had chosen Riverby was its nearness to Roxbury and the home farm.

He always rejoiced when he saw his father's angular, sprawling handwriting on an envelope and turned to that letter first, as he sorted his varied mail. How had he ever thought Pa merely a rough old tyrant? His letters were hard to read, since he wrote without benefit of commas or capitals, one sentence part of the next in a long, tumbling series that someway managed to evoke the very atmosphere of the farm.

Dear Children:

This leaves us all well hoping it may find you both well I received your letter last week it informed me you was well you must write oftener than you do our winter begun early and held on till the fifteenth of this april and then it begun to be warm and saturday 17th the wind got south and it rained a good part of the day on sunday the weather was very warm and the snowdrifts went finely it has drifted so we have not been the deacon road this winter but the drifts are most entirely gone the grass starts finely and I am glad to see it we have had to buy some hay at $16 per ton butter is not worth quite as mutch as I expected we have sold from 51 cents down to 42 cents we have made 8 tubs that weighed 400 lbs we make 100 lb a week we have 18 cows come in and shall have three more by the first of next month our sugar season has been good we have made as mutch as fourhundred weight we have finished today and drawn our things to the house we have got a very good hired man this season the last I herd from Mary jane and homer they was well you and ursula must come home in june about the middle you must come without fail I want some trout and I want to see you very mutch eden has

got a fine hound he got him at baltimore he cost him a
nice little sum of money but he is a nice one I remain
          your affectionate parent Chauncey A Burroughs

This was a cheerful letter, John thought, as he folded it
and put it away, and yet there were signs in it which he
had not liked. The low price on butter, Eden's expensive
purchase—only one of many extravagances he could not
afford. Pa's old firm control and Ma's industry seemed to
be waning. They were growing old, he told himself with
a sigh. More and more the farm seemed to be in the hands
of the boys, who would mismanage it to death one of these
days. Just now Curt seemed to be in the saddle, a short-
sighted dreamer if there ever was one!

By June, John's vague forebodings were apparently to
be realized. A hurried message from Pa begged him to
"come now," and soon he found himself in the midst of a
tangled financial muddle, harder to straighten than any of
his broken banks. Curt's farm on the east end of the main
property had to be sold to satisfy his creditors and to keep
them from foreclosing a mortgage on the main farm.

It was sad to see Pa's worried face and Curt's hangdog
look, but hardest of all to see his mother grieving. How
old she had grown! The evening he came, he saw her standing in the pantry washing a great pile of milk pans, just
as she had washed them for over fifty years; just as she
had washed them when he was a little boy and stood beside her, finding her a fortress of strength, comfort, and
wisdom.

"Let me help, Ma!" he said, taking the dishcloth from
her hands.

As she looked up at him, a mist of tears clouded her eyes. "To think that he's losing all his beautiful back fields . . ."

"I know, Ma—it's hard."

Yielding to a rare impulse, he put an arm across her shoulders and held her for a moment—tight. She looked up at him then with a smile of sudden sweetness, transforming the wrinkles, the haggard, careworn face.

"You've done right well, John. I always knew you would," she said. It was perhaps the only tribute she ever paid him.

Not long after John had returned to Riverby, another harassed letter came from Pa. They had had to assign the main farm to Hiram Meeker, who would certainly take it over unless they could pay a percentage on demand.

Roxbury July 5th 1877

dear son we are all well we are bothered to raise that money you can send your check for six hundred dollars and you can fill out a note to the Hobart bank and in- dorse it they want security we will three of us sine the note I and eden and hiram we will do what is right for you draw the check to the order of hiram Meeker it ought to be here by the middle of next week we are be- ginning to mow today grass is quite good Elder Hewitt has promised us the money this fall then we would pay it back to you it would oblige us very much write back by return mail

your affectionate parent Chauncey A Burroughs

John Burroughs remembered well how a youngster had

once gone shyly out to the barn to ask his father for money to buy an algebra, and been refused. He remembered well how that same youngster grown older had worked all one hot summer at tasks far beyond his strength, thinking that he would be sent to Harpersfield in the fall—till the blow fell. There was no money for "fancy schooling."

It was not so much that he could not help me, as that he did not seem to care, mused John. *But now I can help him.* The thought seemed to give him satisfaction and a curious pleasure. That very day he sent off the check.

It was April 15 of the next year—close to the time of his own birthday—when the greatest joy of his entire life came to John Burroughs. For the miracle happened; a small son arrived to lighten the loneliness of Riverby.

From the first, Julian was a bright, serene, and happy baby, with the Burroughs look plain upon him and eyes that never lost their first brilliant blue. To John he seemed atonement—and promise; to Ursula, the one needed happiness to turn away her bitterness. As they watched and loved the baby, and marveled at his growing, again they found comfort in their love for each other. Now—at last— would Riverby be a home?

The spring of Julian's coming, the spring of John's forty-first birthday, the journal was filled with the sheer zest for life; filled, too, with new activities and interests. He was planting more peach trees, for fruit growing was the main industry of his farm. He was going to Washington on banking matters; he was reading some verse for Gilder, editor of *Scribner's Monthly*, to tell him whether to publish it. He had a new dog named Lark, "a wonderful dog in the woods. . . ." So it went.

It was fall when Amy Kelly came to visit them, to exclaim over everything in the place, but especially to rejoice over the baby. It warmed John's heart to see her rocking him, with all the old look of love and pride on her face. He thought again of his own childhood and the worn blue cradle that was rarely empty.

Whenever little Julian cried, Ma rushed to pick him up, in spite of Sulie's protests. "You'll ruin him, Ma. I'm getting him on a schedule."

But Amy Kelly only snorted, "Schedule! Love never ruined a child, Sulie! Don't forget that!"

What did it mean to him, John wondered, to see his mother holding his own child? It gave him a curious warm happiness, a sense that the past and the present were one, related at last—all mixed up together. The future was a part of them, too.

Strange that as a youngster he had never thought of this— there would be something of his mother, and something of himself which Julian would in turn pass on to his children and his children's children. And long after they were both dead, these distant, shadowy children might speak of them, remembering! A kind of immortality? No, it was more than that. Someway, John felt that he was a part now of the real stream of life; he had found a fulfillment which all the published books in the world could never have given him.

Chapter 15

ONE OF THE REASONS JOHN BURROUGHS CHOSE THE SITE of Riverby was it nearness to the mountains. All his life he had loved them. How often he had seen his mother, when the boys were raucous, or Pa was hurried and rude, go to the door and look up at Old Clump! When she returned, there was peace and gentleness in her eyes. As a boy he had read Old Clump like a book; known its high upland pastures, its rugged dome, the wild cherry trees where the chickadees nested, the deep ledges where the phoebes hid their young.

Looking up from his oars as he rowed on the river, he noted the Catskills, a jagged blue line against the sky, backdrop for the gleaming reaches of the Hudson. It was good to look up at them, to find peace in their solidity and strength. But even more John longed to conquer them, to have the fun and struggle of the climb. Slide, the greatest of them, had tempted him for years; it had been a "summons and a challenge" to him. He had fished the streams that flowed in all directions from its head; he had camped in the wild, lonely valleys at its foot, but the summit had eluded him. Someday, he told himself . . . someday.

Then there came a day in July when Ernest Ingersoll was visiting him, a friend who was both companion and woodsman. The humid heat of the last few days was gone. The air of early dawn was crisp and cool. Slinging their packs into the back of a wagon, they started out behind the old horse. They drove through Esopus and Olive, then turned sharply west on a road that went to the heart of the Catskills. They found at last a lonely farmhouse and an accommodating farmer, who was glad to put their beast up for the night.

But could they find Slide? A shy mountain, John thought, so surrounded by other peaks! King of them all, but someway hiding behind them. From the west it looked like the back and shoulders of a great horse, with its head down, grazing. If it would only lift its head up, it could overlook the world, but some mysterious enchantment kept it bound. The climb up the long, bent neck to the high shoulders would be steep and exciting! Here was the great gash which gave the mountain its name, the long gray mark of the landslide which had stripped away a mane of spruce and balsam for hundreds of feet.

Could they reach it? Hiring the farmer's son as a guide, they struck in by way of Weaver Hollow. But the boy seemed talkative and uncertain, and they sent him back with a ready excuse. As they plunged on, Slide disappeared again and only Wittenberg loomed up before them. Then Wittenberg it must be, and perhaps from its top they could gain a sense of direction for the greater climb.

After a long and desperate struggle through a trailless wilderness they conquered Wittenberg, and here, as John later wrote, the earth fell away at their feet and curved down through an immense stretch of forest till it joined the plain of Shokan, then swept away to the Hudson and beyond. But where was Slide? With his strong, steel-like muscles and slight, fluid body, John climbed swiftly up and up into the top branches of a tall pine. Yes, there to the southwest, the great enchanted horse was peacefully waiting, at least six or seven miles away. John noted the waning light and thought of the small amount of food in his pack. Not this time, he told himself ruefully.

"Here's a good place to sleep," Ernest called, pointing out a thick stretch of moss, soft on the ground between two fallen logs.

"With footboard and headboard all ready!" John answered, wandering away to collect balsam boughs with his hunting knife.

Soon the springy bed of boughs was prepared, with larger branches thrust in at the side to meet and form a canopy overhead, as snug a place as any "runner of the woods" could need. And now the delicious smell of wood smoke. Cold meat, raisins, and water from the canteens. Then silence, broken only by the distant hunting call of a barred owl. The protective custody of the stars.

Coming down the mountain next morning, John, who was ahead of Ernest, suddenly saw a huge brown creature cantering along ahead of him, the biggest porcupine he had ever seen. "Whoa there, Goliath!" he cried, and with his usual curiosity decided he would try to catch him. After all, what was a porcupine like?

Shielding himself with his roll of blankets, he threw himself down on the beast, which seemed to submit peacefully with its tail flat on the ground. A misleading quiet. When John slowly moved his hand to touch the tail, it went up like a trap springing, to fill his wrist full of sharp barbed quills. As he cried out, Ernest came running, and the low-slung creature managed to lumber away. Setting his teeth, and trying to practice Indian endurance, John let the cruel, hooked quills be pulled out one by one.

Now the two men went on down, down, still further down into one of the loveliest valleys they had ever seen. A wild, rushing trout stream foamed beside them, while suddenly the trees stood away and a superb mountain view lay ahead. So lonely and beautiful a spot John marked at once for his own. This was his first view of Woodland Valley, where later he pitched his tent twice that same season, and to which he returned over and over through the years.

It was June of the following year, a month earlier than last time, when John Burroughs started out again for Slide. His favorite friend, Myron Benton from Amenia, was with him and the Van Benschotens, all brave and steady climbers. This time they would try it from Woodland Valley, the hardest and steepest method of ascent. They spent the night in the last clearing, on a farm belonging to a man named Larkins, camping on a stream which came from the very heart of Slide. Surely they could make it from here!

And yet, in spite of himself, John was moved by doubts. He had heard of parties who had tried the climb from this side and returned completely baffled and defeated. Not so easy to stalk an elusive, hidden mountain through six or seven miles of pathless woods.

"The eye is of little use," John said to Myron. "First we'll take bearings, then push boldly up."

"Yes," said Myron, "like fleas on a great, shaggy beast, looking for its head."

Closely they questioned Larkins, who dropped his old felt hat on his kitchen table and, putting first the right hand on one side of it and the left on the other, said, "There Slide lies, between the two forks of the stream, just as my hat lies between my two hands. David will go with you to the forks; then you'll have no trouble."

But Larkins was wrong, though he had climbed over the mountains many times. The peak did not lie between the forks, but exactly at the head of one of them. Early in the morning, with blankets strapped to their backs and food for two days well stowed away, they set out along an old, obscure bark road that kept crossing the stream. A bright, warm morning, with a hint of rain in the gusty wind that blew down from the mountain, carrying the smell of pine needles dried in the sun, or the sharp, heady smell of balsam. No sound from the steady footsteps that followed the old overgrown road through five miles of forest. Then the forks, and three miles later the "burnt shanty," a name merely, since there had been no shanty there for twenty-five years. But the ruthless work of the old bark peelers could still be seen, where the great trunks of virgin hemlocks had been stripped and left to rot, overgrown with wild cherry, in woods now turned to beech and maple.

Loveliest of all was the stream, singing beside them over its gray-green rocks and pebbles. An ideal trout stream, John thought, now loitering, now deepening around a great boulder; white, sparkling, and cold as snow water. Only in remote woods like these could you find a brook in all its original beauty. Civilization had corrupted the streams as it had ruined the Indian!

When they were at the forks they caught, or thought they had caught, through an opening, a glimpse of Slide. But was it the head, or the rump, or the shoulders, if it was Slide at all? Here there was such a maze of underbrush and trees that the way seemed lost, and Larkins' boy had come to the end of his reckoning. But a line of blazed trunks suddenly led them forward; then turning to the left, they began a steep, hard climb.

Here were frequent marks of deer hoofs in the soft earth, or now and then a great clawed gash down a tree trunk which showed that a bear had been at work. No birds, save occasionally a winter wren, darting about and scratching in the leaves. Now a shower plunged down suddenly, and as suddenly stopped. Still they pressed on.

Three hours from the forks they came out on the broad, level back of the mountain, the base on which the peak of Slide was reared. Then they plunged into a great grove of spruce, dim, silent, and weird as any temple of old. Here they paused to eat, finding a little spring gushing from the dark-green moss.

Dramatic contrast to the quiet grove, which now they left, came the next discovery confronting them. Suddenly, as they came from the protection of the spruce grove, there—straight before them—giving them no other choice, stood the high perpendicular battlement of Slide. Up and still up it stretched from the plain on which they stood, like the cruel rock-bound fortress of some ancient tyrant.

Now it was ledge upon ledge and precipice upon precipice, up and over which they made their way with labor and care, zigzagging from left to right, cautiously searching out support for foot and hand. Here on the northern side of the mountain grew moss and lichens; occasionally a stunted mountain ash gave them foothold, or a spruce stood in the way to block them, like some evil genius. Once John put out his hand to catch at a twisted root, but it broke under his clutch and he felt himself sliding into space. Sickness swept over him, a moment of utter panic. But he twisted his body to catch and cling to a young birch tree. Bending under his weight, it still held—and saved him. With the sheer wall of rock below him, he grasped this slender lifeline, and waited . . . till the vertigo passed.

From the top of the mountain they looked down, down, rejoicing over their hard-won conquest. How soft and flowing, John thought, all the outlines of the mountains looked! The forest swept over them like a carpet. To the east, looking over nearby Wittenberg, they saw the Hudson and the land far beyond; to the south, Peak-o'-Moose, with its sharp crest, and Table Mountain, long and flat. In the west, Mount Graham and Double Top, over three thousand feet high; to the north, old Panther and range on range of peaks beyond.

They had left summer, with its full, rich green, below them, but on the top of the mountain they found another season. Here was the painted trillium, and claytonia, flower of April, while far below them the fields held ripening strawberries. They had climbed to spring.

Suddenly Myron Benton held up his hand. "Listen, what bird is that?"

"A thrush," John answered, "but what thrush, I wonder?" he added half to himself. "Not a hermit—I heard one down the mountain. Not the olive-backed . . ."

Flutelike, but delicate and muted, the song went on, like a musical whisper, John thought, of great sweetness and power.

"Let's call it the Slide Mountain thrush," said Myron Benton.

Later John Burroughs knew it was Bicknell's thrush, a southern form of the gray-cheeked thrush, sometimes found on the higher mountains of New York and New England.

It was the tenth of June when the little party dropped down from the mountain, summer by the calendar, but winter now by the bitter wind in their faces and the snow that swirled around them. Cautiously they made their way down the treacherous wall of rock, to claim again the peace and beauty of Woodland Valley. Trout and strawberries, Mrs. Larkins' "cream pot, butter jar and breadbox"— surely the gods coming down from Olympus had no better fare!

Many times after this John Burroughs returned to camp in Woodland Valley or to climb the elusive, dangerous Slide. Years later, when he was fifty-six, he wrote in his journal: "Tramp up Big Indian Valley today, with my roll of blankets on my back. . . . Reach the summit about two and pass the night there. A good time all alone with that sublime view. Porcupines very plenty and annoying at night. I made a nest under a ledge of rocks on the summit and sleep fairly well. A grand view of a storm from seven to eight. Look straight out into its heart of fire."

There have been critics of John Burroughs who have written that he was only a "tame naturalist," a lover of the garden and the hearthside, but these strictures are wrong. The man who climbed up the steep, sheer wall of Slide, who slept alone on its top, who exulted as he looked into the heart of the lightning, was no tame pussycat. The man who fished the wild trout brooks of the Catskills and found his way through the primitive forest was close in spirit to the pioneers from whose loins he came.

Perhaps, of all the memorials remaining to him, John Burroughs would like best the simple rock that commemorates him on the top of Slide Mountain. It reads:

In Memoriam
John Burroughs,
Who introduced Slide Mountain to the world.
He made many visits to this peak and
Slept several nights beneath this rock.
This region is the scene of many of his essays.
"Here the works of man dwindle in the
Heart of the Southern Highlands."

John Burroughs looked up from his desk in the little book-lined study, which he had built on a "bench of land" below the house. Footsteps sounded outside and a merry face came round the doorjamb.

"Hey! How's old Bruin in his cave?"

"Oh . . . Julian. Sucking his paws, boy, sucking his paws!"

As always, the sight of his son gave him a thrill of pride and pleasure. The fat-legged small boy, who only the other day had followed him everywhere, asking a hundred questions without waiting for an answer, was now this tall, restless, energetic youngster, almost ready for college. John noted the muddy shoes, the stained leather jacket, the eager light in eyes which seemed almost too blue in the tanned face.

"See you've had good hunting!"

Julian looked down at his brace of partridge a trifle ruefully. Then he put his gun in a corner and dropped the birds against it. "You don't like these, Father—but Mom will."

"Well, after all, who taught you to shoot?"

"Father, I've found the most wonderful place . . ."

"So that's the exciting news!"

"It *is* exciting. Back in the Black Pond region. I thought I knew every inch of it, but I found . . . well, I was just scrambling along through the woods after some birds— they got away. Then suddenly I was blocked by a kind of rocky cliff, really high, and a great rock stood in front of me, which I climbed. Wow! What a view! Bet I could see four states. Then I looked down below—and there was the loveliest little place. . . ."

"What made it so lovely?"

"Well, the rocky cliffs around it on one side, and the biggest, hoary old hemlocks, and a little bright green marsh, green as—well, the first stand of rye grass in spring."

"Still green in the fall?"

"Yes. I climbed down to look at it. You should see the arbutus leaves round it!"

"What else?"

"It's a place under a spell, Father—really. I settled down there for a moment, half expecting to see the hoofed one and hear the magic pipes. Don't believe anyone had been there in years."

"Sounds marvelous, Julian! Do you think you could find it again? Show it to me? If it's really there, and you didn't dream it. . . ."

"It's real, all right."

Perhaps Julian realized that his coming had been rather a ruthless interruption, for he asked tactfully, as he turned toward the door, "How did the writing go today?"

"Oh, fair—a few pages. The dinnerbell rang three times this morning. I pretended not to hear the first time, but . . . she kept on ringing. It got on my nerves so I had to go. Thought the neighbors would think there was a fire."

"What was the matter?"

"Just a stopped-up sink. Hud could have fixed it faster than I can, but your mother must have her favorite hired man."

"It's really a tribute to you, Father. She thinks no one can do things but you."

"No, she likes to see me doing real work, not loafing over some foolish papers. And it gives her a sense of power to be able to call me."

"You need another retreat, Father, some place further away. Sorry to have added to your woes!"

"You never could, Julian," John Burroughs answered.

Julian recovered his partridges and his gun, then rushed out, banging the door behind him. The lad's going left a vacuum, John thought, as he remembered wistfully the time when he had had the same eagerness and young enthusiasm. For a moment he stared at the papers before him and the pencil he had dropped; he could almost hear the quiet stealing back to fill up the vacuum. Where was that last sentence that had been in his mind? It seemed to be really lost this time.

Had it been a mistake to talk to Julian about his mother's ringing the bell? The boy loved her—wrong perhaps to criticize her—and yet he was the only one to whom he could talk. Almost man-grown now, almost ready for college, more friend and companion than son. He realized the situation—always had been understanding.

It wasn't as if he himself objected to a small chore thrust suddenly under his nose. Heaven knows, he was used to them, had been since he was a boy. He had always liked to work with his hands, with his whole body, too, the way a countryman does. His mind turned back to the year of the three eights, 1888. It was work that had saved him then.

The first excitement over the building of Riverby had gone. There were not many visitors then, except for Walt and Myron Benton. Sulie was lonely—and difficult—wanted him to sell the place, give up writing and move to town.

"But I can't sell," he kept telling her. "It's my life. How can I live in a city?"

It was work that had saved him. Instead of selling his place, he had added to its acreage and gone in for growing grapes in earnest. First the new land had to be cleared, plowed, and harrowed. Then he had set out twenty-four hundred new vines, the good Concords, Delawares, Niagaras, Campbells Early, and other fancy varieties. Two thousand currant bushes between the vines and two thousand hills of raspberries.

Had that been work, or hadn't it? He had stuck with the men, plowing, planting, digging in posts, stringing long wires between them. When the grapes were high, there was all the hard program of spraying for black rot, fertilizing, tying up stragglers, harvesting. And how he had loved it!

In a few weeks his muscles had been hard again. He had slept the instant he fell into bed, eaten like a wolf. From feeling himself "at a low ebb," he had grown vigorous and well. And the "grape racket" had paid. Hadn't it brought him hundreds, yes, thousands of dollars in pure profit every year?

At the end of summer it was a beautiful sight to see the great, shining piles of grapes in the little fruit house—with its hand-carved sign of the grape over the door—ready to be packed and shipped; each variety in its own fancy basket with the seal of Riverby upon it. Yes, he was proud of his grapes! He had succeeded with them.

But now even that first enthusiasm had waned. Grape growing had become a big industry, a bit too mechanized, often burdensome. He was turning it over more and more to Hud Covert and the other hired men, to Julian who understood it and liked to work at it, too.

Yes, his beautiful place, Riverby, had become overorganized of late, and the life of his home, he thought with a

sigh, was little more than domestic tyranny. Must he look
for another escape? And where was peace and freedom to
be found—where but in the beauty of nature and the silence
of the forest?

He pushed his papers away now with a quick, nervous
gesture. No use trying to write; other thoughts were in
command. Soon there would be the supper bell, rung
loudly with its come-hither firmness. Yes, he must go with
Julian to see this magic place in the woods. Endearing of
the boy to like it so much! Had he said there was a stream
running into the swamp?

John shut the door of his bark-covered study and went
to stand for a moment in the rustic summerhouse nearby.
A wonderful spot from which to watch the river in all its
gleaming length, from the Vanderbilt place opposite, to
the dramatic bend of Crum Elbow far to the south. It was
beautiful—but, like Riverby, too restless and too big. "It is
an arm of the sea, and it holds me at arm's length," he had
once written to Walt.

Not until next spring did John and Julian finally go on
their trip of exploration. They hiked west from the railroad station for half a mile along the country road, then
turned suddenly into the woods. For perhaps a mile more
Julian led on through the wild tangle, crushing the fresh
ferns, with their faint, aromatic odor, climbing over wind-
falls, pushing aside hobblebush or alder. Then at last he
pulled back the drooping branch of a hemlock and cried,
"There, Father! See . . . down there!"

John, who had been watching for birds' nests, or studying the ground to find jack-in-the-pulpit or lady-slipper,
came quickly to attention. Straight before them, close

under a high, rocky mountainside, set about with cliffs at one end and with hemlocks at the other, lay a swamp of emerald green. Here and there a second growth of maples covered it, and all about it stood forgotten berry bushes, twisting vines—the wild, unbroken forest.

Soon, like boys of the same age, they were exploring the lovely place, climbing Julian's great, glacier-scarred boulder with its wonderful view to the west, finding the brook, ice-cold and swift-flowing, the deep cave, like some giant's refrigerator thrust in the cliff, and discovering by accident the clear, high echo that drifted back to them from the rocks.

"John Burrrrrrrrrrroughs!" Julian called childishly, and "Rrrrrrrrrows," the old Silurian rocks answered.

So bemused and happy they were, they hated to turn home. Satisfied with the sandwiches they had brought in their pockets, they sat watching the soft, early dusk of the woods creep slowly in, adding enchantment to this place of peace.

"Now," Julian said quietly, "listen! Now for the pipes of Pan!"

But what they heard was only the throbbing, reiterated complaint of the mourning doves and then the sudden, swift insistence of the whippoorwill, so close to them that the staccato "cluck" came clear. A star looked down through the hemlock branches and John rose regretfully to his feet.

"Best go back, Julian."

"Wish we could spend the night."

"We'll come again soon and bring out blankets."

It was a strange coincidence that not many months after this a young farmer of the neighborhood, Amasa Martin, came to talk to John Burroughs. He stood shyly, twisting his hat in his hand, with his brogues turned slightly in, and his black eyes looking straight into John's.

He thought perhaps Mr. Burroughs would be kind enough to help him. He had found a wonderful stretch of land in the woods—it was called the Worthington lot. All he needed was the capital to buy it. He could pay off the money soon with hard work and profit from his vegetables. Part of the land was a muck swamp. If drained, it would be perfect for celery. Amasa's swamp, John soon discovered, was Julian's magic place.

From force of habit, he discussed the matter with Sulie, who was businesslike and practical and had often saved him from some foolish investment. "A peck of nonsense," she cried at once. "You're always hard up, or so you say. Riverby needs repairs now, but you always have money to hand out to any good-for-nothing loafer."

Perhaps this opposition was just what he needed to help him decide. He advanced the money, keeping the swamp and part of the high, rocky cliff as his own share. He was glad to help Dick and Amasa Martin, who were far from being lazy loafers, glad to buy a place of peace and beauty, which might prove beyond price.

The next spring they were literally "skinning the swamp," clearing out the maples, cutting ditches, and blasting an outlet through the west rim of rock. Deep down in the rich black earth they found old logs, which beaver had chewed, a wooden mallet, and a stone bottle unhurt by the passing years. So wild and lonely it seemed, but life had been there before them!

The new effort, the new land to conquer, brought happiness to John. "All day at the swamp," he recorded in his journal of May 1. "Break through the rocky barrier today and let the water out; little leaves the size of mouse ears all around me. How lovely the world looks!"

By fall he was carrying his plans still further. What was land without a home built upon it? With the help of a good workman, he used gray stone from nearby ridges, the "first cut of the logs," slabs with the bark on, from a nearby sawmill, yellow birch from the forest. It was fun to help push up the big stone fireplace, to trim the interior with smooth yellow birch.

Perhaps this cabin in its wild, secluded forest spot, shut away from the restless, noisy world of the big river, might prove the answer to his deepest longing, might in reality be his place of peace.

Through these years John, who kept in loving touch with the farm at Roxbury, had been deeply worried about his brother Hiram. When he went home, he found him sullen, absent-minded, and resentful of his brothers. Once he had caught him pounding at a stanchion in the barn again, as if to release some unbearable tension. From the time when he himself had lived in Washington, bitter letters had kept coming from him.

Roxbury, May 17th, 1877

Dear Brother

Your lecture is at hand. . . . You say if you was here

as I am you would put a different face on things. I would
like to see you do it, but I have been a fool for staying
here as I have. If I had went away when I was of age,
as I ought to have done, I could come back today and
buy the whole of you out and sell them again.

Again I have tried my best to not have Pa get in debt.
Made all their sleds and drags and harrows and a grate
many times furnished my own timber and what do I get
—kicks and cusses. . . .

Roxbury, June 25th, 1878
Well, John, I am completely discouraged there is no
use of my staying here and fooling my time away when
I can't have a voice in anything whatever. . . .

Feb. 6th, 1882
I don't take any comfort here and I am going to get clear
of them. . . . Come up the first of March. Write.
Res'p yours,
Hiram

Poor Hi! Of all his brothers, John had loved him the
best, and he felt the deepest pity for him. Yes, he should
have run away at the time he planned to go West and the
old carpetbag lay under his bed, ready and waiting for the
trip. He had been a dreamer, too conscientious—and too
timid.

Amy Kelly died two years after little Julian was born,
but she had seen the baby, John remembered with joy.
After that Pa had grown gentler, more subdued, indiffer-
ent. Soon he, too, had slipped away. Now Eden had mis-

managed the farm, until John, who held a controlling interest, had insisted that Hiram be given his chance.

From '83 to '89 Hiram came into his own and struggled to make a go of things, with the result—complete and total failure. It was December when John had had to go to Roxbury to tell his oldest brother that the farm could be his no longer. When he arrived at the village lawyer's, no Hi was there to keep his appointment; no one knew where he was. But John guessed by instinct and found him hiding at Eden's. The stark lines in his journal showed the bitterness of this moment.

"Up early. Hiram in a hurry now to get home. We walk across the mountain through wind and snow. As we toil up the mountain, I note how troubled and careworn he looks. He stoops as if bearing a great burden. My heart bleeds for him. I know how he is weighed down, but nothing can be done. He has lost the battle; the old farm and home he cannot keep.

"I spend a week in Roxbury, trying to sell or rent the place and let Hiram stay there. Must keep a home for Hi there, if possible."

It was the summer of the work at the swamp, when Hiram, homeless and poor, came to Riverby. To John it was a great joy to have him come, and with all his heart he longed to offer him a permanent home. But from the first, Ursula was cold, distant, almost openly hostile.

"That little nubbin of a man going to stay here?"

"Sulie, he's my brother. Where else should he stay?"

"Not in this house."

"But, Sulie . . ."

"Not at my table! I'll not have him eating in my clean kitchen. He's dirty, John!"

In the end he had to yield, putting his brother up in the fruit house and carrying his meals out to him in the bark-covered study, even washing his dishes, since Ursula refused to do it. It was pitiful to see Hiram receiving the tray meekly, as if he were some nameless tramp begging at the door. John could not bear it.

"What's too good for him is too good for me," he cried hotly to Sulie, and took his own meals in the study with Hiram from that time on. He thought then of the lonely retreat in the woods. In building a house there, might it not be a home for Hiram, too?

It was December when the cabin was finished. On Christmas Day a group of friends came from Poughkeepsie to celebrate the opening of "Slabsides," to light the first fire in the big stone fireplace, to pull the new latchstring, which from that time on was always "out" to so many friends—to the famous and the obscure, to the merely curious and the genuine nature lover, to clubs and school groups, to photographers, artists, and editors—to all the many men, women, and children who came to pay tribute to the writer, John Burroughs, and even more to the man.

The next May, when it was warm enough, Hiram arrived to stay, bringing his bees and bee traps, and John moved out to the cabin in the woods to set up housekeeping with him. A cheerful letter went off to Myron Benton:

Now for two weeks I have been living at Slabsides. . . . My brother Hiram is with me and we are quite comfortable and happy. I like it so well that I may stay most of the summer. The quiet, the seclusion, the wildness and the freedom from domestic tyranny, are like balm to my spirit. . . .

We have set out 30,000 celery plants and shall put out many more. . . . When can you come over and taste the hospitality of Slabsides? I can give you a good bed and plenty to eat, and a hearty welcome. Come, and stay several days.

At last John Burroughs had found a new freedom and a place which he could really share with his friends.

Chapter 16

JOHN BURROUGHS' JOURNAL SHOWED A NEW ZEST FOR life that spring when he first moved to Slabsides.

"I feel like a toad when he escapes from under the harrow," he wrote. "I look about me and find life worth living, after all. Hiram is a great help just by his presence. . . . Celery begins to grow rapidly."

The simple uncluttered cabin, surrounded by the impersonal beauty of the forest, brought balm to the spirit of the man, burdened by too many cares. Days held the timeless quality now which long ago he had loved as a boy, fishing the shining trout streams with Granther. He could saunter as he wished, or sit and dream, or work upon the new book on Whitman—his eleventh book, which he was trying hard to finish—or find outlet for his energy hoeing the rich black soil between the light-green rows of lettuce and celery.

Hi, grizzled and slouchy, puttered about, tending to his beehives, or searching for the eggs which his chickens hid between the rocks, anywhere they chose to lay them. At night, after a dinner cooked in the fireplace, the two men settled comfortably down for a long, peaceful evening in front of the "singing hickory logs," while Silly Sally, the cat, purred a pleasant accompaniment from John Burroughs' knee.

Sometimes they shared their common memories, talking about hired men they had known, or the time Hiram "sassed" back a teacher; the fun they had taking apples to the Gould cider press, or that cold October night when old Cuff killed a giant coon. The glamor of the past, the strange, wistful charm of a lost childhood! Sometimes they shared the deeper companionship of silence.

Two men, as unlike as men could be; a world of experience and knowledge stood between them. One was without education, never looked in a book, was without mental keenness or curiosity, never asked about the writing which was his brother's life. The other a world traveler, friend of many learned men; self-taught and widely read; lover of books and all that books could give; a keen critic of literature, science, and philosophy; one of the finest craftsmen of his time.

Yet there was no sense of strain or difference between them, closely bound as they were by the tie of blood and the bond of a deep affection. For John Burroughs, no matter what the years had brought him, had never gained an artificial veneer, or the sham growth of self-conceit.

Often in the morning, though he hated to leave the woods, John hurried down to Riverby to cast a watchful eye upon his grapes, collect his huge bundle of letters from the post office, and sometimes, if the cook allowed it, to rifle the ample larder of the stone house. It was hard to resist Sulie's wonderful pies, cakes, and hot bread.

But the letters were often disturbing, filled as they were

with requests for autographs, or interviews, or magazine articles, or even for lectures, which would pull him away from this peaceful life into the strain and excitement of some great occasion. Just before coming to Slabsides, wasn't it, he had gone to speak on Whitman before the Phi Beta Kappa Society of Yale?

"Dreadfully scared and worried as usual," he had written in his journal. "But when the hour strikes and I find myself face to face with the enemy, my courage and confidence mount. . . . A fine audience and appreciative."

One of his earliest guests at Slabsides was the famous western naturalist, John Muir, a powerful, long-legged Scotsman of tremendous energy and caustic wit. Being used to a listening audience himself, John found it something of a strain to be always on the receiving end of a monologue which was constant, fluent, and unrestrained. Yet he enjoyed Muir and the two "Johnnies" became fast friends.

Of all the guests who streamed in upon Slabsides that first summer, perhaps the girls of Vassar's Wake Robin Club were the most welcome. Bright-eyed, eager, and with some real interest in nature, led by their teacher, Miss Whitney, who was a serious student of bird lore, they had visited him even before the building of his cabin, and now were ecstatic over it.

Like curious chickadees they swarmed over the little house, praising the furniture made by John himself, with its spiral twists and knots, the blue bed coverlets which Amy Kelly had dyed and woven, the smoky iron kettle on the hearth, the latchstring hanging at the front door, and its curiously twisted wooden knob. Most of the girls settled down on the floor to listen respectfully as he talked, but one girl chose his breadbox as a seat, giving it, from that time on, a permanently warped personality!

"Birds jest can't act natcher'l, when so many females go round peerin' at 'em," was Hiram's comment; and, indeed, it was with a combination of pleasure and relief that John helped to pick up all their belongings, from hairpins to handkerchiefs. Chattering and joyful, they wandered off down the woodland trail, looking in their bright, receding dresses like flowers on the march, he thought to himself, as he waved them good-by.

All through the summer months Hi and John camped together at Slabsides, till the cold of late November came to end the long idyl. Hiram chose a Catskill town for the winter, and John returned to Riverby, though he was well aware that he would probably be left in sole possession of it. Sulie had taken to wintering in Poughkeepsie of late, and once more Julian would be torn between the two of them.

"Hi leaves me today to be gone several months," John wrote at Thanksgiving time, "thus closing a curious and interesting chapter in my life. . . . He never looked into one of my books lying here on the table. When my Whitman book came, I said to him, with the book in my hand, 'Hiram, here is the book you have heard me speak about as having cost me near four years' work, and which I rewrote about four times.' 'That's the book, is it?' said he, but he never showed any curiosity about it, or desire to look into it."

Another year—another season. John Burroughs tapped the maple trees for sap, driving in the spiles and catching the precious juice in buckets, as he had done almost every year since childhood. Now he sat outdoors by the sap pans, boiling the syrup down to sugar, enjoying the ancient ritual, gazing off now and then at the glassy blue length of the Hudson. It was so calm that he could see the dim reflections of the gulls as they winged their way upriver.

The edge of April, his favorite month for . . . how many years? His birthday month. The calendar said sixty-four, but calendars were meaningless. Soon he was back at Slabsides, giving the cabin a spring cleaning which even Sulie might have approved, but not forgetting the really important things—to hunt for arbutus under the leaves of the forest, or to note the fresh yellow of marsh marigolds, or the joyous, looping flight of a goldfinch. And Julian, just back from Harvard for his spring vacation, came hiking out to climb the cliffs with him, hunt for the eagle that sometimes perched on a high, dead tree, or cook a juicy steak over the coals.

Through these days of spring with all its duties and joys, and with its constant stream of mail from all sections of the country, one series of letters made a deep impression on John Burroughs. They came from an unknown woman admirer of Middletown, New York, where he had once worked as receiver of a broken bank.

Dear Mr. Burroughs:
    I am yielding to an impulse, often suppressed before, to tell you how sincerely grateful I am for my share in

the messages you have sent from time to time to your unknown friends.

I can't call myself a stranger—I've known you nearly eleven years, and we have so many friends in common! I suppose I ought to mention the most aristocratic ones first—the orchid family, several members of which summer in this locality—but there are a host of others, even the plebeian skunk cabbages, that we are both intimate with, so why pretend to apologize on the ground of being a stranger? . . .

Sincerely, gratefully yours,
Clara Barrus M.D.

State Hospital, Middletown, N. Y.

This first letter was a long one, full of originality, and John was intrigued. Women correspondents were no novelty to him. He had had many of them, from Mary Burt, who started using his books in the schools of Chicago, to Ida Tarbell, his latest valued acquaintance.

But this was new, this was refreshingly different! Even in the middle of Julian's Harvard commencement, when the boy graduated *cum laude*, announcing his engagement to Emily Mackay of Cambridge at the same time—even at this busy moment, John stopped to write to his new friend.

It was late September on a gray, forbidding day when Clara Barrus climbed off the train at West Park to greet the man whose books she had known and loved. A small, agile woman with light-brown hair, whose eyes gazed up into his blue-gray ones with a look of undisguised warmth and admiration.

"So you are here—really here?" he cried, then looked characteristically down at her shoes to see whether she was equipped for roughing it. Soon she was walking beside him along the country road, then following over the steep woods trail and up a rough stairway cut in stone, acquitting herself so well that he smiled at her with approval.

Now they were exchanging experiences before a roaring fire, discussing everything from orchids to Tolstoy. She had read all his books, he found; not only read them, but knew them well. To make her even more welcome, she was a great admirer of Whitman. The hours sped briskly by, as they shared a delicious meal of broiled chicken, roast potatoes, and onions.

A little over a month later he returned her visit by calling on her in the State Hospital at Middletown.

I am so glad I made the visit and saw your own place and in that delightful little room. How nicely you have feathered your nest, and what a charming nest! . . . Now I am beginning to be conscious of a great loss in not having known you years ago or when you first began to love my books. All the beautiful springs and summers that are past, and you not a part of them for me! I shall have the pleasure of sending you a copy of my collection of Nature poetry.

Still later he wrote:

Your note about the *Songs of Nature* came last night. How sharp your eyes are! I should never have seen one

of those errors and omissions. I shall write them to the
publishers today. . . . If you will allow me, I will send
you all my proof in the future.

So began a lasting friendship with "C.B.," a brilliant
woman who was nature lover and critic, and, on the practical side, an excellent typist as well. Since she repeatedly
begged to help him, he took her at her word. Soon she was
preparing his manuscripts, reading galley proof, criticizing
and editing. Through the years she became companion,
secretary, and friend, accepted and liked by all the Burroughs' household. When Julian and Emily moved out of
the little brown cottage which John had built for them and
went to manage Colonel Paine's estate "up the river," then
C.B. came to live in it and make it her home. And nothing
that she did ever seemed to change the first impression of
her, which John's journal revealed. "The most companion-
able woman I have yet met in this world—reads and de-
lights in the same books I do—a sort of feminine counter-
part of myself."

For many years John Burroughs had known Theodore
Roosevelt. In his early days of ranching out West, the
young Roosevelt had written to ask natural-history questions and Burroughs had answered them.

Once Roosevelt wrote from England to say that he had
happened upon a book of Burroughs there and the mere
sight of it made him "desperately homesick."

Then in 1900 young Teddy Roosevelt, just eleven years
old, came to visit Slabsides for two weeks. Burroughs, who

liked boys and was "Uncle John" to most of them, found
that he really had his hands full this time. "Led me a chase,"
"terrific energy," "such a reckless climber I thought the lad
would break his neck," "his father in miniature" were some
of the descriptions which he used afterwards.

Not only to Teddy Roosevelt, but to hundreds of young
people all over America, John Burroughs had become the
beloved interpreter of "all outdoors." They read his
sketches in their favorite magazines, in *St. Nicholas*, and
Youths' Companion; they found the most fascinating of
them in their own school readers. They wrote to him, long
questioning letters, or to thank him for his books.

"Dear John Burroughs," one country boy wrote, "I got
your book through the mail, marked on the wrapper second-class matter. But it isn't second-class matter. I have
read it and it is first-class matter. The binding and the
make-up may be second class, but the matter is first-class."

Not only magazine articles and books, not only the fact
that he was included in school readers, but also the work
of the Burroughs Nature Club, of which he was president,
made the naturalist known to an immense and constantly
increasing audience. This was a national organization, with
branches in many of the schools and a central governing
body in New York City, which included distinguished
scientists of the American Museum of Natural History,
Dallas Lore Sharp, and Raymond L. Ditmars, Curator of
the Department of Reptiles of the New York Zoological
Park.

In view of the fact that Burroughs had become an authority, it was natural that he should be seriously disturbed

over a new trend in the country, a growing number of books apparently concerned with natural history, but based on a grossly false and inaccurate picture of it. These books were popular and exciting; but, as Burroughs felt, they were misleading the young people. "Nature fakers," he called the authors who wrote them; two men in particular were the chief offenders. Did no one have courage enough to speak out against them?

At last he could restrain himself no longer. With all the power of a pen usually known for its gentleness, he wrote a scathing and red-hot article. "Real and Sham Natural History" was published in the *Atlantic Monthly* of March, 1903, to launch a minor hurricane overnight.

"Only an honest book can live; only absolute sincerity can stand the test of time." "To treat your facts with imagination is one thing; to imagine your facts is another."

Of course the men attacked rose to defend themselves, and their friends rallied round them, while editors, publishers, and scientists, with papers in *Science* and other magazines, hastened to support Burroughs. Among the most ardent of these supporters was the hard-hitting Theodore Roosevelt. It was at this time that the long acquaintance between the two men ripened into a deep and lasting friendship.

One March day at Slabsides, John sat sorting his mail at the rustic table which he had built himself. The usual collection of letters, bills, invitations; some fiery comments on his recent article; a woman in Albany writing to ask whether she had "seen a fox sparrow"; a boy out West sending a description of a "queer nest"; between the last

two a big, square, impressive white envelope with the stamp
of the White House across its top. Tearing it open, he held
an invitation from Roosevelt to join him on a trip to the
Yellowstone, if, it added, the Senate would let the President
go in the face of all the fuss the yellow papers were making
over his hunting. The letter continued with an alluring description of the Park, the various wild animals they might
see there, and ended with a promise to protect Burroughs
from all undue weariness.

John read the note over again, excited and pleased. He
snorted a bit when he reached the reference to "weariness."
Did the President think he was old? Only four years before,
he had been on the Harriman Expedition far up in Alaska,
almost to the Arctic Circle. Forty scientists in every field,
from John Muir, the "mountain and glacier man," to
Fuertes, the famous bird painter. Came back stronger than
when he left. Old!

Even in the midst of his excitement, other thoughts came
flooding in. The edge of April at Slabsides—all the beauty
of the new earth. Plants to be set and watched—warblers
returning. How long would he be gone? Weeks probably!
To leave the place he loved best in the world, and go
careening across the country—where was the gain? How
great the loss!

All his life John Burroughs had been torn between two
desires, the love of home and the love of adventure, like
the little boy who had run away on the Deacon road, only
to turn back again. How could he leave Slabsides now? For
a long time he hesitated, looking out the window at the
leafless trees, where new life, deep within, was already be-

ginning to rise and flow. Then he put out his hand to take the cattail quill.

March 10th, 1903

Dear President Roosevelt:

It is more than kind of you to ask me to go with you to the Yellowstone Park this spring. Of course I should like to go, if there are no "ifs" in the way. I am no chicken and seem to be able to tramp and climb mountains as well as ever I could. I don't kill game . . . but can eat my share of it. Hoping the "yellow papers" will not cheat you of your outing,

Your loyal friend and supporter,
John Burroughs

It was April 1 when, after dinner and a good night's rest at the White House, John Burroughs found himself riding down Pennsylvania Avenue at the right-hand side of the President. The place of honor, the lines of cheering people, the sense of adventure, all were a heady brew of excitement and pleasure for the quiet naturalist. And as he rode, the vigorous, smiling man beside him seemed to vanish. Another time, another Washington came flooding back, vivid and clear—a tired, lonely man in an old-fashioned barouche, surrounded by cavalry with sabres drawn; on the sidewalk, in the wartime throngs, an unknown, penniless lad with all the years before him.

Lincoln. He had given his life that this country might endure. In a sense, this moment, this hour of prosperity, these people cheering a powerful new leader, were a heritage from the great martyr-president. Whitman, he thought, would have seen that! And suddenly, with irresistible yearning, he longed for Whitman. His friend, his beloved Walt, eight years dead—but deathless, he knew now, forever immortal.

As for himself, he thought humbly, what mystery of life and time had decreed that he should be riding here at the right hand of Roosevelt? "All the honors that have come to me have been an undeserved surprise."

City after city, state after state—the long presidential special careened across the country. Baltimore, Pittsburgh, Madison, Chicago—at every station or whistle stop the President was called upon to speak. At night in some big city a welcoming procession and political banquet.

Tension, fatigue, long hours, excitement. Traveling with Roosevelt, John thought, was like being at the center of some national emergency. But he enjoyed it, for all that. As for himself, he was feted and lionized almost past enduring, and made to feel that he was welcomed for his own sake.

At St. Paul, as the presidential procession crawled through cheering lines of people, a crowd of school children surrounded his carriage to give him a huge bouquet of flowers. At the dinner in Minneapolis, a distinguished-looking stranger approached him with outstretched hand. "Not just that you're the President's friend," the man said as he greeted him, "but because *you are you* we are happy to have you with us! You, John Burroughs, have given more pleasure to more people in this room than Roosevelt ever has—or ever could give," he added.

These were glamorous days for John Burroughs. The

hours of riding through wild western country; the sight of strange birds and animals, from the pygmy owl to elk and mountain sheep; stopping to whip the water of the Yellowstone and pull out the big cutthroat trout, named for the yellow mark across their front. Sometimes John seemed to feel the shadowy form of Granther standing beside him, as he landed a "big un."

Then the campfire at night, with the line of hills black against the sky and the flames leaping high. At these times the President grew boyish, even hilarious, as he told tales of ranch life, of days with the Rough Riders, or even more lurid stories of his experiences as police commissioner of New York City.

It was late in April when John left the President's party at Livingston. No, he wasn't going home yet. The West and adventure were in his blood now.

"Soon I'll be at the ranch of Abe Gill in Montana," he wrote home. "I shall see a phase of life and nature that I have long wanted to see . . . maybe I'll buy a ranch and become a cowpuncher." At sixty-six John Burroughs was still following his Deacon road.

By the end of May the traveler was home again, not averse to a little peace after all the strenuous wandering. His first thought was of how to return Roosevelt's hospitality. A letter went off to the White House from the cabin in the woods. Would the President and his wife come to spend a week in Slabsides, bringing young Teddy along with them?

Soon the answer came. Sometime after the Fourth of July the President would be happy to accept the invitation,

though only for a day. Young Ted could not make it, but Mrs. Roosevelt would come.

On July 10, John and Julian stood on the dock at Riverby, watching the President's yacht come up the river. They waved, and the boat changed its course, heading toward them. Then the President appeared on deck, in white linen and straw hat, with his wife beside him. A small naphtha launch brought them ashore, and immediately Roosevelt noticed a group of workmen who had gathered and were standing at one side, quietly watching.

"May I meet your friends, Oom John?" he said.

"Mr. President, this is Charlie Burger who fought in the Civil War."

"Ah—you were in the big war; I was in the little one!"

Disdaining any carriage, Mrs. Roosevelt joined the men, and soon they were walking through the coolness of the forest, with special enjoyment since the day was hot. John hesitated when he came to his sharp, steep short cut, but Mrs. Roosevelt managed "breakneck stairs" cut in the rocks as well as the rest of them.

The little house in the woods, with the old hemlocks and the high, towering cliffs beyond it, the delicious lunch—chicken and onions and potatoes, with homemade cider; the clear, ice-cold water from the spring—filled the Roosevelts with genuine enthusiasm.

As the hours moved on and they finally started to leave, the President's wife turned to look at the cabin with a lingering, wistful glance. "Such peace and beauty here, Oom John!" she said. "Even at Oyster Bay we never find such blessed quiet."

"I wish you could stay to hear the whippoorwill and other night sounds . . ."

"With all my heart I wish we could," she answered.

Now Mrs. Burroughs appeared in her finest rustling silks, ready with horse and phaeton to drive Mrs. Roosevelt to Riverby. A party in the stone house—neighbors to meet —some of Sulie's most delicious food—the long anticipated day was over.

As John and Julian stood on the dock, watching the *Sylph* take its smooth way downriver, Burroughs said, half to himself, "A wonderful man, son, always on equal terms with the greatest, but never holds himself above the humblest. How I wish Walt could have known him!"

Through the years the friendship continued, with interchange of letters, with visits at Oyster Bay and Pine Knot, Virginia. And Roosevelt showed his warm admiration for John Burroughs by the dedication in his book: *Outdoor Pastimes of an American Hunter.*

To dear Oom John
It is a good thing for our people that you have lived,
And surely no man can wish to have more said of him.

Chapter 17

T̲ʜ̲ᴇ̲ ʏᴇᴀʀꜱ ᴘᴀꜱꜱᴇᴅ; ɪᴛ ᴡᴀꜱ C̲ᴀʟɪꜰᴏʀɴɪᴀ, ɪɴ F̲ᴇʙʀᴜᴀʀʏ, 1921.

The last log stretched across the firedogs broke suddenly and fell into the fire with a hissing sound. Slowly the fire died. Cold, John Burroughs thought—always cold—and tried to hitch his chair closer—a little more warmth and brightness! The big logs were too heavy to handle, but if he could reach the poker . . . Cautiously he bent forward, aware of weakness and uncertainty; now . . . now . . . his trembling fingers touched the top of the iron. With the malevolence of the inanimate, it fell from his grasp and clattered on the hearth.

"C.B.," he called petulantly, "C.B." But no answer came. Half anxiously he peered around the wing of his big chair. Where was everyone? Had they left him alone, sick and miserable as he was? Only the shadows seemed to move closer. Then he remembered—gone to take those silly visitors to the train. So many people always coming to call, asking questions, trying to make him talk—stupid, foolish questions. Except Sandy Smith. Strange to find old Sandy out here! Used to go to school with him in the West Settlement schoolhouse.

He leaned his head back against the chair, closing his eyes for a moment and letting the years drift by. Sandy wasn't good at wrestling as Jay Gould had been. What fun they had had at school! Old Oliver used to try to make him write—couldn't do it! Softly he chuckled to himself.

The school seemed to vanish and suddenly the walls of the Washington station closed about him—dark and filled with drifting grayness. Out of the mist a proud, young figure came toward him, tripping down the steps of a train, rushing forward. A big yellow market basket on her arm, her face was alight with a lovely, welcoming smile.

"Sulie!"

"Johnny, see—I've brought you some of my best new preserves!"

Dear Sulie! She had been a fire in his blood once, but the years had built barriers between them—disillusion and heartbreak. No, they had done it themselves—why blame the years? Dead now—so long dead—but he loved her. He would always love her.

He opened his eyes and again the room came in focus— the cluttered mantel top, the fallen poker, the feeble fire. Suddenly, with an overwhelming longing, he wanted to go home.

People had been kind to him; kind of Henry Ford to send up that new car from Los Angeles, but—he wished he hadn't come. "Get him away from New York State cold," they said; "nice warm winter in California." Warm! This was a damp chill that crept into his bones, caught in his throat till he thought he could never be warm again. And the dripping rain forever falling from the eaves, blinding the windows.

This little cottage near Pasadena was better than La Jolla had been. At least he was away from the ugly, gray, pounding sea, from the waves that never would rest, and the rushing traffic. Away from those hideous yawping seals, forever barking on the rocks. They called this place "The Bluebird"! Humph! No bluebird would be caught dead in it.

He wanted to see Julian and Julian's children, Betty and John—especially Betty, his first beloved grandchild. What a gay little thing she had been! He had named his camping place at Woodland Valley for her—Camp Betty, he called it—and young John who would carry on the name.

Home—he wanted to go home—to see Old Clump again, to watch the brown soil turn to a reddish-rose color under the spring plowing, to put his own new seeds in the straight furrows, to hear the first call of the whitethroat . . .

Spring—it would be here soon—he must go home. His restlessness rose suddenly to a state of panic. "C.B.," he called sharply, "C.B." A lovely young face came round the wing of his chair and looked down at him; a gentle arm slid round his shoulders. His granddaughter, another Ursula.

"Why, Baba, what's wrong? Shall I build up the fire for you?"

"I thought you had gone, too!"

"Mercy, no, I'm staying to take care of you."

It was February 17th when they took John Burroughs to the hospital as he sadly said, "None of my people ever stayed in a hospital." He had been there four weeks when at last, after giving him a little time to gain strength, they put him on the train for the East.

The stateroom was filled with friends, doctors, attending nurses, loaded with farewell gifts and flowers. Too solicitous, too noisy! "Good-by—thank you—yes, indeed—good-by."

Lying back in his berth, weak and incredibly tired, he watched with vague detachment the long, wind-marked ridges of the desert slide by, mile on mile, mile on mile. Though it was March, the heat of June seemed to beat upon him. The even bumbledy-bum, bumbledy-bum of the train was soothing; as he closed his eyes, it crept into his dreams.

When the train stopped at Albuquerque, a sense of dread flooded over him. "Where are we, C.B.? Where am I now?"

"Still in New Mexico, but we're making good time."

"Three thousand miles from New York. C.B., do you really believe I'll live to get home?"

"Now, now . . . don't let yourself . . . !" She smiled at him, trying to be reassuring. Suddenly he glared at her, with fury in his heart; then turned sadly away. He was an honest, forthright man—always had been. Why couldn't she tell him the truth?

When they reached the prairies, some of John's desperate fear lessened. This was land he knew. Still the West, but here he felt at ease. Those months when he had taught near Chicago, he had loved the flat land with its high, arching dome of sky.

Wistfully he watched from his window as the big farms changed places, moved slowly by each other across the landscape, like pawns side-stepping on a giant chessboard. Now a farmhouse just ahead came rapidly closer, while one behind it, in the distance, seemed to travel with the train—so far one could see on these level, fertile prairies.

At Chicago he made the change of cars bravely, carried on a stretcher to his waiting stateroom. Again the place was filled with well-wishers and friends, exclaiming over him, begging him to "break his trip" and "stay a bit to rest."

"No, no," he cried with sudden desperation, fearful that C.B. would be moved by the suggestion. "Kind of you, but I must be getting home."

As they left Chicago, new life seemed to flow in his veins, new strength return to him. Almost gaily he asked Clara Barrus to show him his garden catalogues. "Make a list for me, C.B.! I'm going to plant peas early this year; just as soon as we get back."

"Safe, is it?"

"May be nipped, but it's worth a gamble."

"Are we going straight to Roxbury?"

"First to see the family; then back to my beloved Woodchuck Lodge, so near the old farm! Wasn't it wonderful of Ford to buy back the farm for me?"

"What shall I order?"

"Oh, Early Dwarf—or Telephone."

When the train approached Toledo, Ohio, and Ursula

and C.B.'s two young nieces came in to see him, John Burroughs seemed stronger. Propped up against his pillows, he smiled as he stretched out a thin, white hand to his granddaughter's and clung to it for a moment.

"By two o'clock tomorrow we'll be home," he cried with assurance, almost with gaiety in the tone. "Tell C.B. to come here, will you? Want to get that little matter for *Harper's Magazine* straight."

At midnight the old weakness and fear had flooded back. Though he twisted and turned in his berth, there seemed to be no position of comfort, no place of rest. His throat ached, his bones were burning with fever. The impersonal noise of the train was beyond enduring.

At two o'clock he cried out and C.B. came quietly in out of the shadows. Stooping over him, she asked, "What can I do to help you? Let me change your pillows!"

She slid a firm arm under his shoulders, supporting him gently, easing the pillows to smoothness.

"C.B.," he cried, a light flaring up in his blue-gray eyes, "how far am I from home?"

There came a gasp . . . and a long sigh. The eyes closed, the head fell back against her arm. It was over . . . the struggle was ended.

How far from home? And who could answer?

No man had ever loved life, with all its pleasure and sorrow, more than John Burroughs. No man had ever captured more of its richness and joy. No man had ever shared that richness more fully with others. Now he was a wayfarer on the lonely, mysterious road from which no man returns.

At the top of the highest peak of the Catskills, with nothing between it and the sky, there lies a great gray stone with an inscription on it to "John Burroughs, who introduced Slide Mountain to the world."

On the wall of a room in the American Academy of Arts and Letters, to which only the greatest artists and writers belong, there hangs a handsome portrait by Rouland of the man to whom in 1916 the Academy awarded its rare gold medal "for excellence in essays and belles-lettres," not given again for many years.

At the lower end of Manhattan, Public School 188 is called the Burroughs School. In the auditorium, proudly displayed, are his head and shoulders in bronze, bearing the words, "To understand nature is to gain one of the greatest resources of life."

In front of the Art Museum of Toledo, Ohio, there stands a life-sized statue of him by the sculptor, Pietro. At its unveiling, twenty thousand school children passed by in review, waving flags and bearing flowers.

In a quiet bird refuge at Fairlane, the beautiful estate of Henry Ford at Dearborn, Michigan, a small bronze statuette by the same craftsman commemorates the great naturalist. The fountain below it and the walks that lead to it are all made from stone, brought from the farm at Roxbury.

And in a high, lonely field, on the land which he knew and loved as a child, is the most meaningful memorial of all, the big rock where long ago he dreamed his wistful dreams of greatness.

Here, at the edge of April, on his own birthday, they laid his body to rest in a grave beside the rock, where he had listened to the call of the vesper sparrow and looked off to the eastern hills—to the high, sloping fields that "run down from the sky into Montgomery Hollow."

It was a strangely assorted crowd that stood at his burial, the well-known and distinguished, Edison and Ford, Edwin Markham, the poet, and the plain people, who perhaps understood him best. Without adornment or ostentation the simple grave remains, with only the bronze by Pietro to mark its place—a bas-relief of John Burroughs, the seer, gazing into the distance, with a hand over his eyes.

In summer the closed gentian and silverrod bloom in the field beside the grave and the wild clematis sends a shower of white over the stones. All summer long the visitors come quietly to pause beside it; farmers with their children, or passers-by from the big city. To each in his turn the place has a different meaning.

To those who can understand, John Burroughs might say: In the strain and fever of life do not forget to turn back to your mother, the earth; for from her comes strength—strength for the body, and strength for the soul. "The most precious things in life are near at hand, without money and without price. Each of you has the whole wealth of the universe at your very door. All that I ever had, or still have, may be yours by stretching forth your hand and taking it."

Bibliography

Barton, William E. *Lincoln and Whitman*. Bobbs-Merrill Co., 1928.

Barrus, Clara. *The Heart of Burroughs' Journals*. Houghton Mifflin Co., 1928.

—— *John Burroughs, Boy and Man*. Doubleday, Page & Co., 1920.

—— *The Life and Letters of John Burroughs*. 2 Vols. Houghton Mifflin Co., 1925.

—— *Our Friend John Burroughs*. Houghton Mifflin Co., 1914.

—— *Whitman and Burroughs, Comrades*. Houghton Mifflin Co., 1931.

Beard, Charles A. and Mary R. *The Rise of American Civilization*. The Macmillan Co., 1934.

Brooks, Van Wyck. *The Times of Melville and Whitman*. E. P. Dutton & Co., Inc., 1947.

Burroughs, John. *In the Catskills*. (Selections from his writings, with photographs by Clifton Johnson.) Houghton Mifflin Co., 1911.

—— *My Boyhood*. (With conclusion by his son, Julian Burroughs.) Doubleday, Page & Co., 1922.

—— *Notes on Walt Whitman as Poet and Person*. American News Co. of New York, 1867.

Canby, Henry Seidel. *Walt Whitman, an American*. Houghton Mifflin Co., 1943.

Charnwood, Godfrey Rathbone Benson (1st baron). *Abraham Lincoln*. Henry Holt & Co., 1917.

Foerster, Norman. *Nature in American Literature.* The Macmillan Co., 1923.

Garland, Hamlin. *John Burroughs.* The Century Magazine, Sept., 1921.

Haring, H. A. *Our Catskill Mountains.* G. P. Putnam's Sons, 1931.

—— *The Slabsides Book of John Burroughs.* Houghton Mifflin Co., 1931.

Johnson, Clifton. *John Burroughs Talks.* Houghton Mifflin Co., 1922.

Kennedy, William Sloane. *The Real John Burroughs.* Funk & Wagnalls Co., 1924.

—— *Reminiscences of Walt Whitman.* Alexander Gradner, England. David McKay, Importer. Phil. 1896.

Masters, Edgar Lee. *Walt Whitman.* Charles Scribner's Sons, 1937.

More, Carolyn E. and Griffin, Irma M. *The History of the Town of Roxbury.* The Reporter Co. of Walton, N. Y., 1953.

Osborne, Clifford H. *The Religion of John Burroughs.* Houghton Mifflin Co., 1930.

Perry, Bliss. *Walt Whitman.* Houghton Mifflin Co., 1906.

Thomas, Benjamin P. *Abraham Lincoln.* Alfred A. Knopf, Inc., 1952.

Whitman, Walt. *Leaves of Grass.* First Edition, Brooklyn, 1855.

—— *Specimen Days in America.* Walter Scott, London, 1887.

Wiley, Farida A. *John Burroughs' America.* Devin-Adair, 1951.

LIST OF BOOKS BY JOHN BURROUGHS

Notes on Walt Whitman as Poet and Person, 1867
Wake-Robin, 1871
Winter Sunshine, 1875
Birds and Poets, 1877
Locusts and Wild Honey, 1879
Pepacton, 1881
Fresh Fields, 1884
Signs and Seasons, 1886
Indoor Studies, 1889
Riverby, 1894
Whitman, a Study, 1896
The Light of Day, 1900
Literary Values, 1902
The Life of John James Audubon, 1902

Far and Near, 1904
Ways of Nature, 1905
Bird and Bough (poems), 1906
Camping and Tramping with Roosevelt, 1907
Leaf and Tendril, 1908
Time and Change, 1912
The Summit of the Years, 1913
The Breath of Life, 1915
Under the Apple Trees, 1916
Field and Study, 1919
Accepting the Universe, 1920
Under the Maples, 1921
The Last Harvest, 1922

Notes and Acknowledgments

NOTES

Chapter 15, on the climbing of Slide Mountain, is based on John Burroughs' own account, as given in "The Heart of the Southern Catskills," a chapter in his book *Riverby*.

The analysis of the Civil War in Chapter 12 is based on the present author's own book, *The Railroad to Freedom*.

Chapter 16 is based in part upon John Burroughs' book, *Camping and Tramping with Roosevelt*.

ACKNOWLEDGMENTS

First of all I wish to express thanks to Elizabeth Burroughs, oldest grandchild of John Burroughs, who has answered all my questions with patience and kindness and given me many vivid pictures of her grandfather's life.

Also to the late Julian Burroughs, son of John Burroughs, who gave me permission to make use of the facts in his book, *My Boyhood*.

Also to Miss Farida Wiley of the American Museum of Natural History, New York City, Secretary of the John Burroughs Association.

I am indebted to Houghton Mifflin Co. for permission to use the letters from John Burroughs to his wife Ursula, also the correspondence with Clara Barrus, as published in *The Life and Letters of John Burroughs* by Clara Barrus, Houghton Mifflin Co., 1925.

I am grateful to Mr. Edmunds and Mr. Graham of the Ford Company Archives at Fairlane, Dearborn, Michigan, for giving me access to the original Burroughs material in their files.

To the officials of the Manuscript Room of the Library of Congress for permitting me to study the galley proof of John Burroughs' first book, *Notes on Walt Whitman as Poet and Person,* as well as other original material.

To the officers of the American Academy of Arts and Letters of New York City for giving me access to their collection of Burroughs' manuscripts and clippings.

I am greatly indebted to Mr. Wilson Burroughs and to Mrs. John C. Burroughs for allowing me to spend a week end at "Woodchuck Lodge," John Burroughs' summer home at Roxbury, N. Y., as well as for showing me in person much of the naturalist's beloved childhood farm. I am also in debt to Mrs. Burroughs for the original letters from Chauncey to John Burroughs.

And to the following persons for giving me information, as well as their own individual insights and impressions of their famous fellow-townsman: Mr. Ralph S. Ives, Mrs. Olive McLaurie, Mr. Thomas A. Porter, Mr. and Mrs. Bruce Caswell.